Celebrate the Months
OCTOBER

EDITOR:
Joellyn Thrall Cicciarelli

ILLUSTRATORS:
David Christensen

Darcy Tom

Jane Yamada

PROJECT DIRECTOR:
Carolea Williams

CONTRIBUTING WRITERS:

Trisha Callella	Kim Jordano
Rosa Drew	Mary Kurth
Marguerite Duke	Melissa Mangan
Ronda Howley	Jody Vogel

TABLE OF CONTENTS

SPECIAL DAYS

FUN FORMS

INTRODUCTION

Seasons, holidays, annual events, and just-for-fun monthly themes provide fitting frameworks for learning! Celebrate October and its special days with these exciting and unique activities. This activity book of integrated curriculum ideas includes the following:

MONTHLY CELEBRATION THEMES

▲ **monthly celebration activities** that relate to monthlong and weeklong events or themes, such as Pumpkins, Fire Prevention Week, and National Popcorn Month.

▲ **literature lists** of fiction and nonfiction books for each monthly celebration.

▲ **bulletin-board displays** that can be used for seasonal decoration and interactive learning-center fun.

▲ **take-home activities** that reinforce what is being taught in school, encourage home–school communication, and help children connect home and school learning.

SPECIAL-DAY THEMES

▲ **special-day activities** that relate to 15 special October days, including Scarecrow Day, Picasso Day, and Columbus Day. Activities integrate art, songs and chants, language arts, math, science, and social studies.

▲ **calendar cards** that complement each of the 15 special days and add some extra seasonal fun to your daily calendar time.

▲ **literature lists** of fiction and nonfiction books for each special day.

FUN FORMS

▲ a **blank monthly calendar** for writing lesson plans, dates to remember, special events, book titles, new words, and incentives, and for math and calendar activities.

▲ **seasonal border pages** that add eye-catching appeal to parent notes, homework assignments, letters, certificates, announcements, and bulletins.

▲ **seasonal journal pages** for students to share thoughts, feelings, stories, or experiences. Reproduce and bind several pages for individual journals or combine single, completed journal pages to make a class book.

▲ a **classroom newsletter** for students to report current classroom events and share illustrations, comics, stories, or poems. Reproduce and send completed newsletters home to keep families informed and involved.

▲ **clip art** to add a seasonal flair to bulletin boards, class projects, charts, and parent notes.

SPECIAL-DAY CALENDAR CARD ACTIVITIES

Below are a variety of ways to introduce special-day calendar cards into your curriculum.

PATTERNING

During daily calendar time, use one of these patterning activities to reinforce students' math skills.

▲ Use special-day calendar cards and your own calendar markers to create a pattern for the month, such as regular day, regular day, special day.

▲ Number special-day cards in advance. Use only even- or odd-numbered special days for patterning. (Create your own "special days" with the blank calendar cards.) Use your own calendar markers to create the other half of the pattern.

▲ At the beginning of the month, attach the special-day cards to the calendar. Use your own calendar markers for patterning. When a special day arrives, invite a student to remove the special-day card and replace it with your calendar marker to continue the pattern.

HIDE AND FIND

On the first day of the month, hide numbered special-day cards around the classroom. Invite students to find them and bring them to the calendar area. Have a student volunteer hang each card in the correct calendar space as you explain the card's significance.

A FESTIVE INTRODUCTION

On the first day of the month, display special-day cards in a festive setting, such as a pumpkin display. Invite students, one at a time, to remove a card and attach it to the calendar as you explain its significance.

POCKET-CHART SENTENCE STRIPS

On the first day of the month, have the class dictate a sentence to correspond with each special-day card. For example, on Teddy Bear Day you might write *On this special day, we celebrate the birthday of Theodore Roosevelt.* Put the sentence strips away. When a special day arrives, place the corresponding strip in a pocket chart next to the calendar. Move a fun "pointer" (such as a pencil with a paper bear taped to it) under the words, and have students read the sentence aloud. Add sentences to the pocket chart on each special day.

GUESS WHAT I HAVE

Discuss the special days and give each student a photocopy of one of the special-day cards. (Two or three students may have the same card.) Have students take turns describing their card without revealing the special day. For example, a student may say *This is the day we celebrate a famous Spanish painter's birthday.* Invite the student who guesses Picasso Day to attach the card to the calendar.

TREAT BAGS

Place each special-day card and a small corresponding treat or prize in a resealable plastic bag. For example, place a mask in a bag for Marvelous Masks Day. On the first day of the month, pin the bags on a bulletin board near the calendar. Remove the special-day cards from the bags and attach them to the calendar as you discuss each day. As a special day arrives, remove and explain the corresponding bag's contents. Choose a student to keep the contents as a special reward.

LITERATURE MATCHUP

Have students sit in two lines facing each other. Provide the members of one group with special-day cards and the members of the other group with books whose subjects match the special-day cards held by the other group. Invite students to match cards and books, come forward in pairs, and introduce the day and book. Display the books near the calendar for students to read.

MINI-BOOKS

Reproduce numbered special-day cards so each student has a set. Have students sequence and staple their cards to make mini-books. Invite students to read the books and take them home to share with family members.

CREATIVE WRITING

Have each student glue a copy of a special-day card to a piece of construction paper. Invite students to illustrate and write about the special day. Have students share their writing. Display the writing near the calendar.

LUNCH SACK GAME

Provide each student with a paper lunch sack, a photocopy of each special-day card, and 15 index cards. Have students decorate the sacks for the month. Invite students to color the special-day cards and write on separate index cards a word or sentence describing each day. Have students place the special-day cards and index cards in the sacks. Ask students to trade sacks, empty the contents, and match index cards to special-day cards.

SPECIAL-DAY BOX

One week before a special day, provide each student with a photocopied special-day card, an empty check box or shoebox, and a four-page square blank book. Ask each student to take the box, book, and card home to prepare a special-day box presentation. Have students write about their special day on the four book pages and place in the box small pictures or artifacts relating to the day. Ask students to decorate the boxes and glue their special-day cards to the top. Have students bring the completed boxes to school on the special day and give their presentations as an introduction to the day.

PUMPKINS

Nothing says October like a fat, orange pumpkin! Pumpkins are gourds that grow on vines and are related to the squash. They can weigh up to 800 pounds (363 kilograms)! Use the following pumpkin ideas to teach your students some exciting, "well-rounded" pumpkin lessons!

LITERATURE LINKS

The All Around Pumpkin Book
by Margery Cuyler

It's Pumpkin Time!
by Zoe Hall

Mouse Paint
by Ellen Stoll Walsh

Our Pumpkin
by Rozanne Lanczak Williams
(CTP)

The Pumpkin Patch
by Elizabeth King

Pumpkin, Pumpkin
by Jeanne Titherington

"PUMPKIN PATCH" BULLETIN BOARD

To form a pumpkin patch and sky, cut a wavy line horizontally through a piece of brown butcher paper (to be the ground) and staple it to the bottom of a blue butcher-paper background. Cut fence posts and rails from corrugated cardboard and staple them along the pumpkin patch. Invite each student to tear a pumpkin shape from orange construction paper. Then have students tear black facial features and a brown stem for their pumpkin. Staple the pumpkins on the fence and in the pumpkin patch. Staple green yarn from pumpkin to pumpkin to make a vine. Staple green construction-paper leaves along the yarn. Add the heading *Welcome to (teacher's name)'s Pumpkin Patch!*

MATERIALS
▲ brown and blue butcher paper
▲ corrugated cardboard
▲ orange, black, and brown construction paper
▲ green yarn
▲ green construction-paper leaves
▲ scissors
▲ stapler

PUMPKIN LIFE CYCLE

Invite each student to color and cut out the flower, small pumpkin, and large pumpkin from the Pumpkin Life Cycle reproducible. Give each student a pumpkin seed and a 24" (61 cm) piece of green yarn. Have students tape the seed to one end of the yarn, and then tape the yellow flower, the green pumpkin, and the orange pumpkin on the string. Have each student place the string of objects in a lunch sack (which represents the ground) and pull out the seed so it is hanging just over the top of the sack. Show students how to pull the yarn (starting with the seed) and say each stage of the pumpkin's life cycle as the reproducible pieces are pulled out of the sack. Invite students to bring the sacks home to share with family members.

PAPER SACK JACK-O'-LANTERNS

Invite each student to stuff a large paper grocery sack half full with newspaper. Have students glue and twist the top of the sack to form a stem. Ask students to paint the sack orange and the "stem" green. When the paint dries, have students paint a black face on the "pumpkin." Curl green curling ribbon and invite students to tie it around the stems to form vines. Display the pumpkins on a piece of brown carpet or butcher paper to represent a garden. Make a sign for the garden that reads *Pick-a-Pumpkin Pumpkin Patch.*

PUMPKIN FINGER PAINTING

Have each student use their fingers to paint an orange and black pumpkin on a large sheet of finger-painting paper. (Tempera paint turns to finger paint when you spray the finger-painting paper with a squirt of starch before students begin.) Ask students to cut out their pumpkin and glue on a brown construction-paper stem. Invite students to curl green pipe cleaners and tape them to the pumpkin stems. Reproduce the song below for each student. Have students learn and sing the song, cut it out, and glue it next to their pumpkin. Display the pumpkins for all to admire.

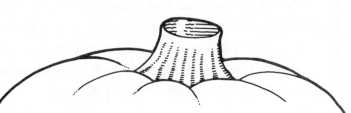

Pumpkin Time

(to the tune of "Are You Sleeping?")
I like pumpkins, I like pumpkins.
Round and fat, round and fat.
See them growing on the vine.
I can't wait to go pick mine.
Pumpkin time, Pumpkin time.

PUMPKIN MATH AND SCIENCE BOOK

Invite each student to cut out the Pumpkin Book Pages and staple them together to make a book. Divide the class into groups and give each group a pumpkin. For page one, have students estimate how much string is needed to go around their pumpkin, cut a piece of string to that length, place the string around their pumpkin, and record the results. For page two, have students estimate, count, and record the number of lines on their pumpkin. Then invite students to estimate their pumpkin's weight. Invite a volunteer from each group to place its pumpkin on a bathroom scale. Have students record their estimates and answers on page three. For page four, ask students to predict if their pumpkin will float and then place it in a tub of water to test it. Finally, invite students to complete page five. For extra fun, invite groups to draw faces on the pumpkins with markers or give away the pumpkins at the end of the day.

FIVE LITTLE PUMPKINS FINGERPLAY

Have each student take home the Five Little Pumpkins reproducible. Give students at least one week to practice the fingerplay at home until they have mastered it. Invite each student to perform the fingerplay on a designated day.

PUMPKIN LIFE CYCLE

I'm a flower.
Color me yellow.

I'm a new pumpkin.
Color me green.

I'm a ripe pumpkin.
Color me orange.

Pumpkin Math and Science

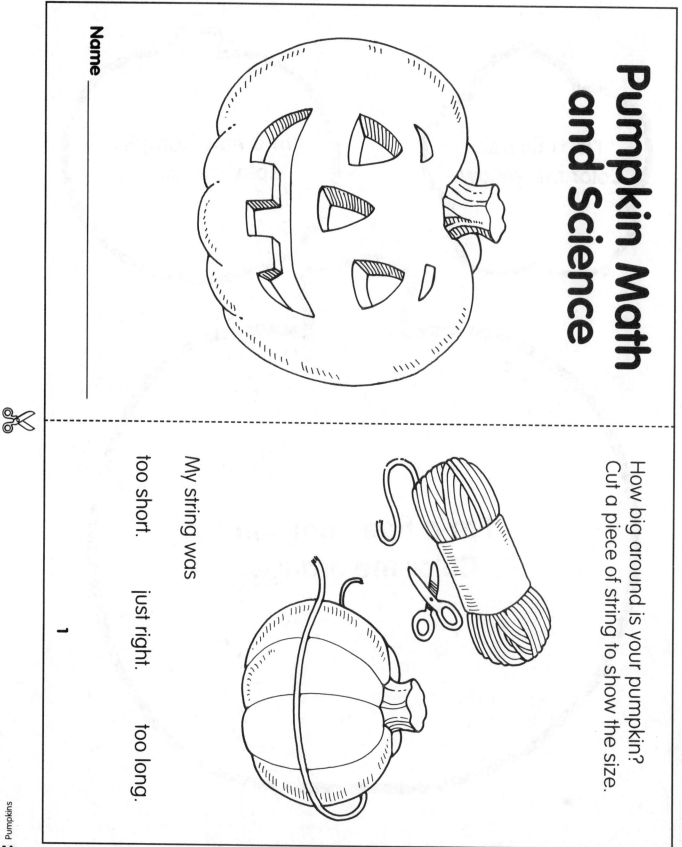

Name _____

How big around is your pumpkin?
Cut a piece of string to show the size.

My string was

too short.   just right.   too long.

1

PUMPKIN BOOK PAGES

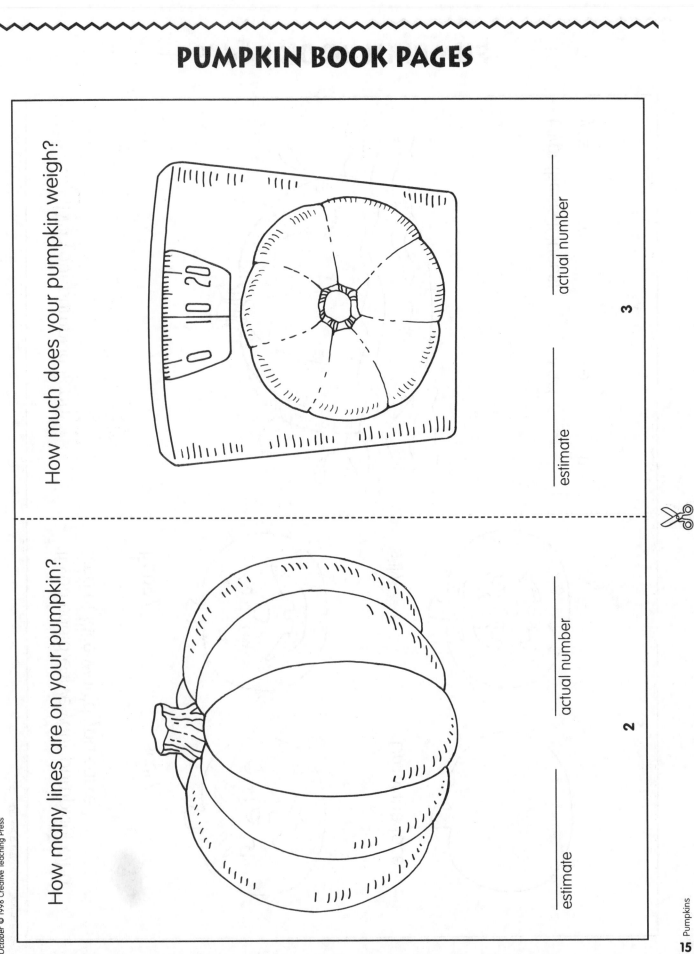

How much does your pumpkin weigh?

_____ _____
estimate   actual number

3

How many lines are on your pumpkin?

_____ _____
estimate   actual number

2

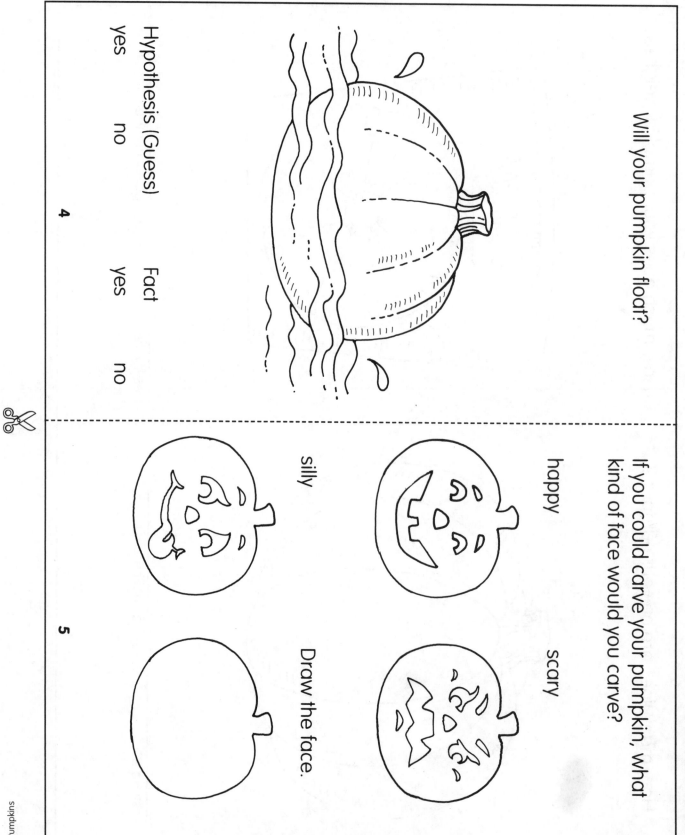

Will your pumpkin float?

Hypothesis (Guess)

yes   no   Fact

yes   no

4

If you could carve your pumpkin, what kind of face would you carve?

happy   scary

silly   Draw the face.

5

October © 1998 Creative Teaching Press

FIVE LITTLE PUMPKINS

Five Little Pumpkins

Five little pumpkins sitting on a gate.

First one said, "Oh my, it's getting late."

Second one said, "There are leaves in the air."

Third one said, "But we don't care!"

Fourth one said, "Let's run and run and run."

Fifth one said, "I'm ready for some fun."

"Oooh," went the wind.

Out went the light.

And the five little pumpkins rolled out of sight.

Motions

Hold up five fingers.

Tap finger on wrist.

Flutter hands down like leaves.

Shake index finger.

Run fingers on palm.

Shake belly as if laughing.

Move hands from left to right.

Pull imaginary light string.

Make rolling motions with hands.

FIRE PREVENTION WEEK

Second Week of October

Fire Prevention Week is a nationally recognized observance designed to educate the public about and increase awareness of the dangers of fire. Help your students learn to become "fire safe" with the following activities—they're hot!

LITERATURE LINKS

Fire! Fire!
by Gail Gibbons

Firefighters A to Z
by Jean Johnson

Henry Explores the Mountains
by Mark Taylor

Lewis the Firefighter
by Harriet Ziefert

The Little Fire Engine
by Graham Greene

Safety Counts
by Joel Kupperstein (CTP)

Safety First!
by Eugene Baker

Don't 4 get 2 STOP and

STOP, DROP, AND ROLL BULLETIN BOARD

Teach students the "stop, drop, and roll" technique for putting out fires on clothing and skin. Then prepare a rebus bulletin board as a reminder. Cut a stop sign from red butcher paper and staple it to the left side of a bulletin board. For the word *drop*, cut a hand from tan construction paper and a vase from blue construction paper. Cut apart the vase so it looks broken and staple the hand above the vase in the center of the bulletin board. Staple the word *and* to the right of the hand and vase. Then cut a dinner-roll shape from white construction paper and staple it to the bulletin board. To make a headline, add the words *Don't 4get 2 . . .*

MATERIALS
- ▲ red butcher paper
- ▲ blue, tan, white, and yellow construction paper
- ▲ scissors
- ▲ stapler

FIREFIGHTER HELMETS

Invite each student to fold a piece of red construction paper in half lengthwise. Have students use scissors to round the open corners of the paper. Ask students to cut a "tail" from the fold, as shown. Instruct students to unfold the paper and push up the "helmet" from the tail. Invite students to write their name on the helmet and wear the helmets as they listen to a firefighter story such as *Firefighters A to Z* by Jean Johnson.

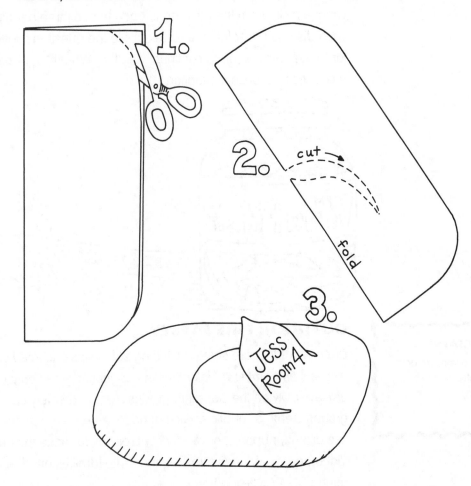

FIRE SAFETY SONG

Teach, and have students practice singing, the following song. Invite students to perform the song for families or for other classes.

Fire Safety Song
(to the tune of "Twinkle, Twinkle, Little Star")

Listen now, this is no joke.
Before a fire, there's always smoke.
If you smell it, go outside.
Never find a place to hide.
Stay down low and crawl away.
Fire trucks are on the way!

"WHAT IF" JAR

Write a "what if" situation for each student on individual slips of paper. "What if" situations could include *What if your clothes were on fire? What if you smell smoke and see it coming under your bedroom door? What if your neighbor's house is on fire? What if you see someone playing with matches? What if you notice a frayed appliance wire at home? What if you accidentally burn your hand?* Place the slips of paper in a jar and have the class sit in a circle. Invite a student to choose a slip from the jar, read it, and choose three people to give an answer. Then discuss fire safety issues related to the question. Have that student pass the jar to the next person to continue. Use the "What If" Jar until each student has had a chance to choose a situation.

OUTDOOR FIRE SAFETY

MATERIALS

▲ video camera/blank cassette
▲ VCR/TV

Discuss outdoor fire safety, including safety tips such as *Pour water on fires, Bury all coals and embers, Make fires in designated areas only,* and *Do not burn trash or leaves.* Divide the class into groups. Assign a safety tip to each group and have groups create a "public service announcement" for the safety tip. Invite groups to use drama, puppets, or mock news reports to make their announcements. Videotape the announcements and invite families or other classes to view them during Fire Prevention Week.

MAJOR CAUSES GRAPH

Write across the top of a large butcher-paper graph the major causes of home fires: careless smoking; heaters, ovens, and other appliances; matches and open flame; electrical shorts; hot objects such as fireplace embers; and fumes such as gasoline spills. Have each student think of a way to prevent one of the problems and write his or her suggestion on a flame, color the flame, and cut it out. Ask each student to tape the flame under the cause and explain the suggestion. Hang the graph during Fire Prevention Week as a fire-safety reminder.

MATERIALS

▲ large butcher paper graph
▲ permanent markers
▲ Flame (Clip Art, page 96)
▲ crayons or markers
▲ scissors, tape

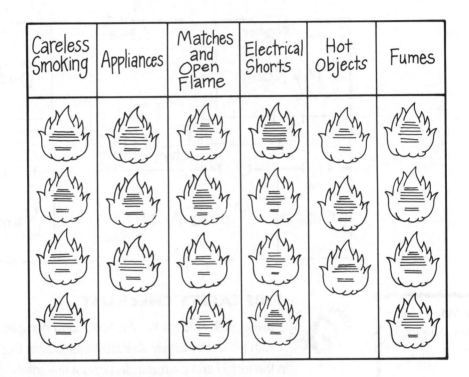

FIRE PREVENTION CLASS BOOK

Read aloud *Firefighters A to Z.* Discuss fire safety and brainstorm as a class a fire-safety tip for each letter of the alphabet, such as ***Always have an escape plan,*** ***Beware of smoke,*** and ***Change smoke detector batteries regularly.*** Assign a safety tip to each student and ask him or her to design a construction-paper book page for that tip. Bind the pages in a class book titled *Fire Safety A to Z.*

MATERIALS

▲ *Firefighters A to Z* by Jean Johnson
▲ white construction paper
▲ crayons or markers
▲ bookbinding materials

MATERIALS
▲ 12" x 18" (30.5 cm x 46 cm) white construction paper
▲ crayons or markers

ESCAPE PLANS

Discuss the need for at-home fire drills and escape plans. Explain that it is best to have two avenues of escape, ladders for houses with two stories, and a meeting place outside the home so all family members can be counted. Invite each student to draw on construction paper a floor plan of one floor of his or her home. Ask students to draw two escape routes from their bedroom to an outside family meeting place. Remind students of alternate exits, such as windows, patios, or porches. Invite students to take their escape plans home and share them with parents.

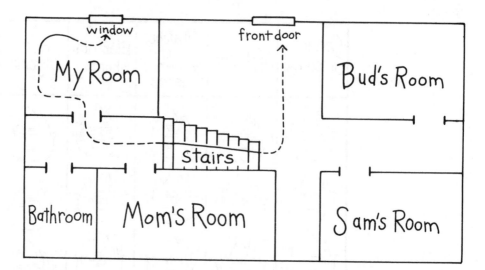

FIRE SAFETY CHECKLIST

Invite each student to take home and complete a Fire Safety Checklist with his or her family. Ask students to post the checklist so everyone in the family can be reminded about fire safety.

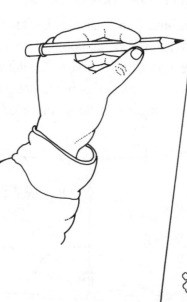

FIRE SAFETY CHECKLIST

☑ Know how to call 911.
☑ Know how to call the fire department.
☑ Know your address and phone number.
☐ Have at least one fire extinguisher in the house.
☐ Have at least one smoke detector in the house.
☐ Find two escape routes from each room.
☐ Be sure lamp and appliance cords are not frayed.
☐ Do not overload electric outlets.
☐ Be sure every fireplace has a screen.
☐ Cook with adult supervision only.
☐ Stock baking soda for kitchen fires.
☐ Put matches and lighters out of children's reach.
☐ Turn pot handles away from the edge of the stove.
☐ Be sure adults use ashtrays and never smoke in bed.
☐ Keep all trash, paper, and flammable liquids away from the furnace and water heater.
☐ Be sure everyone knows how to stop, drop, and roll.

FIRE SAFETY CHECKLIST

- ☐ Know how to call 911.
- ☐ Know how to call the fire department.
- ☐ Know your address and phone number.
- ☐ Have at least one fire extinguisher in the house.
- ☐ Have at least one smoke detector in the house.
- ☐ Find two escape routes from each room.
- ☐ Be sure lamp and appliance cords are not frayed.
- ☐ Do not overload electric outlets.
- ☐ Be sure every fireplace has a screen.
- ☐ Cook with adult supervision only.
- ☐ Stock baking soda for kitchen fires.
- ☐ Put matches and lighters out of children's reach.
- ☐ Turn pot handles away from the edge of the stove.
- ☐ Be sure adults use ashtrays and never smoke in bed.
- ☐ Keep all trash, paper, and flammable liquids away from the furnace and water heater.
- ☐ Be sure everyone knows how to stop, drop, and roll.

BONY BONANZA

October is the perfect time for some skeleton study. Help your students learn about this important human body system and have some fun as they complete the following activities—they'll tickle your students' funny bones!

LITERATURE LINKS

The Bones Book
by Stephan Cumbaa

A Book about Your Skeleton
by Ruth Belov Gross

Funnybones
by Janet and Allen Ahlberg

Nate's Treasure
by David Spohn

The Skeleton inside You
by Philip Balestrino

*Skeletons! Skeletons!
All about Bones*
by Katy Hall

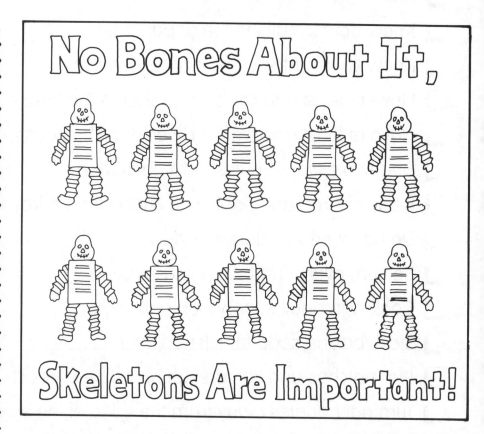

No Bones About It, Skeletons Are Important!

"NO BONES" BULLETIN BOARD

Have student groups look for "bone facts" in nonfiction books about bones. Ask each group to write five facts on scrap paper and set the paper aside. Invite each student to cut a pear-shape skeleton head and a rectangular skeleton body from white construction paper. Ask students to glue the head to the body. Then have students accordion-fold four strips of white paper to make arms and legs and glue them to the rectangle. Invite students to cut hands and feet from white construction paper and glue them to the skeleton. Ask each student to write on the skeleton body the bone facts his or her group collected. Cover a bulletin board with black butcher paper and add the heading *No Bones About It, Skeletons Are Important!* Invite groups to share their facts and hang the skeletons on the bulletin board.

MATERIALS
▲ nonfiction books about bones (see Literature Links)
▲ scrap paper
▲ 12" x 18" (30.5 cm x 46 cm) white construction paper
▲ 1" x 12" (2.5 cm x 30.5 cm) strips of paper
▲ scissors
▲ markers
▲ black butcher paper

BONY BONANZA CUT-OUTS

MATERIALS

▲ colored butcher paper
▲ skeletal-system poster, overhead transparency, or illustration
▲ crayons or markers
▲ scissors

Invite student pairs to trace each other's bodies onto colored butcher paper. (Students can lie in a variety of positions while being traced.) Ask students to observe a skeletal-system poster, overhead transparency, or illustration and draw a skeletal system inside their tracing. Ask students to label at least five major bones and cut out the tracings. Hang the cut-outs along the hallway and add the heading *Bony Bonanza!*

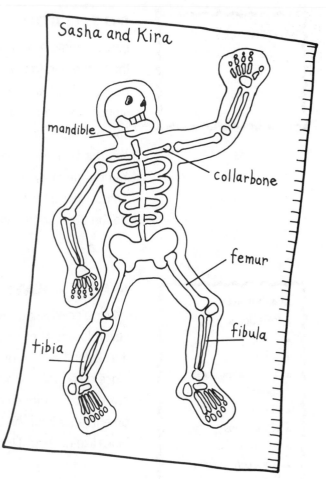

WHITE-STRAW SKELETONS

MATERIALS

▲ 4 ½" x 6" (11.5 cm x 15 cm) black construction paper
▲ white straws
▲ white crayons
▲ glue

Invite each student to use white crayon to draw a simple skeleton on black paper. Ask students to draw the skeleton in an interesting position such as running, placing the hands on the hips, or sitting in a chair. Have students cut white straws into different lengths and glue them over the crayon to represent bones. Display the straw skeletons near the heading *Boning Up on the Skeletal System!*

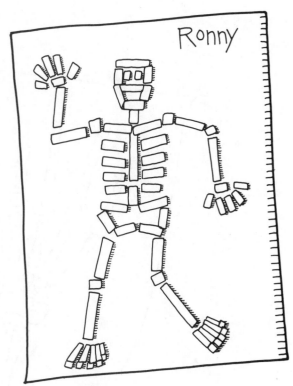

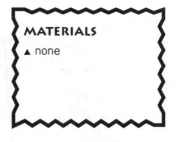

MATERIALS
▲ none

DO THE BONY BONY

Play a variation of "The Hokey Pokey" to teach the skeletal system. Teach students the name and location of major bones such as the skull, femur, fibula/tibia, collarbone, radius/ulna, patella, spine, metacarpals, and metatarsals. Have students stand in a circle and sing the following lyrics:

You put your (skull) in, you take your (skull) out.
You put your (skull) in, and you shake it all about.
You do the Bony Bony and you turn yourself around.
That's what it's all about!

Do the Bony Bony until all major bones have been reviewed.

MATERIALS
▲ tablecloths
▲ aprons
▲ x-rays
▲ overhead projector
▲ spoon
▲ bleach
▲ plastic cups
▲ cotton swabs
▲ black construction paper

MAGIC X-RAYS

Use tablecloths, aprons, and close adult supervision for this exciting activity. Obtain several x-rays from a doctor and display them on the overhead projector. Discuss the skeletal system and the x-rays. Then invite students to make their own "x-rays." Place a spoonful of bleach in a cup for each student. Ask students to dip a cotton swab into the bleach and use the cotton swab to draw an x-ray of a body part or an entire skeleton on black construction paper. (The bleach will fade the paper so it looks like an x-ray.) Hang the papers under the heading *X-ray Vision.*

LABEL THE BONES

Read aloud and discuss a nonfiction book about the skeletal system. Then invite students to complete the Label the Bones reproducible.

Answers:

1. skull
2. mandible
3. collarbone
4. ribs
5. spine
6. radius and ulna
7. femur
8. patella
9. fibula and tibia
10. ankle bone

Silly message: Skeletons are important because they give our bodies form so we don't flop around.

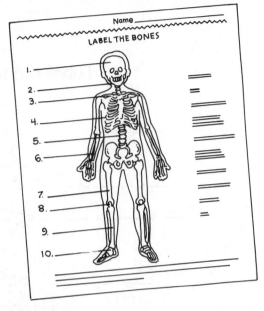

RECYCLED SKELETONS

Send home with each student a Recycled Skeleton Letter, 14 white pipe cleaners, and two white plastic bottle caps. Invite students to follow the letter's directions and make a bottle-cap skeleton with their families. Ask students to bring the completed skeletons to school on a designated day. Display the skeletons near the heading *Recycled Skeletons*.

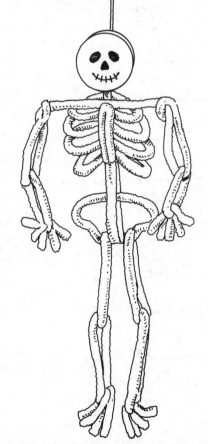

LABEL THE BONES

Label the following bones.

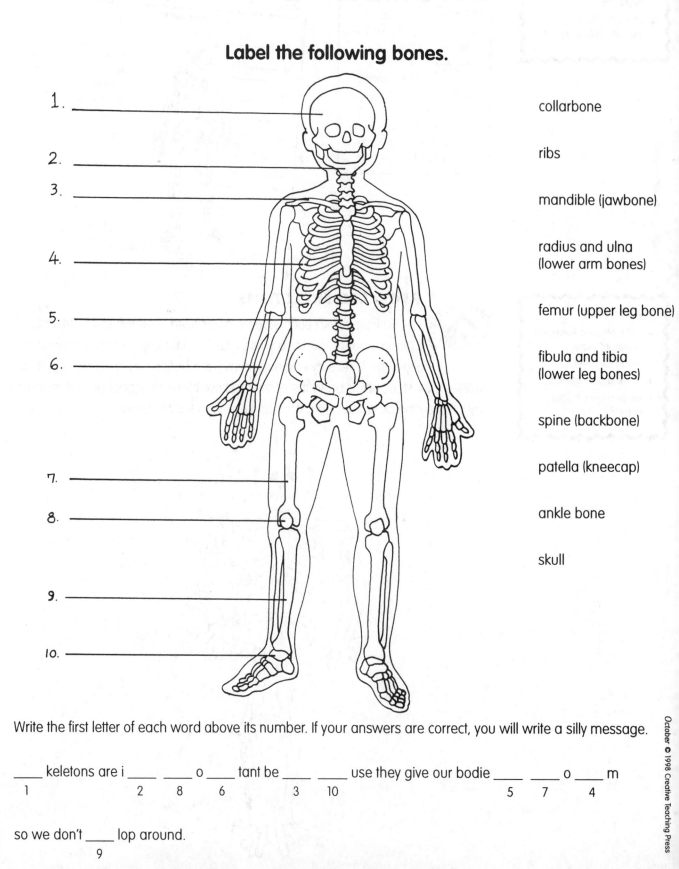

1. _____

2. _____

3. _____

4. _____

5. _____

6. _____

7. _____

8. _____

9. _____

10. _____

collarbone

ribs

mandible (jawbone)

radius and ulna
(lower arm bones)

femur (upper leg bone)

fibula and tibia
(lower leg bones)

spine (backbone)

patella (kneecap)

ankle bone

skull

Write the first letter of each word above its number. If your answers are correct, you will write a silly message.

____ keletons are i ____ ____ o ____ tant be ____ ____ use they give our bodie ____ ____ o ___ m
  1   2   8   6   3   10   5   7   4

so we don't ____ lop around.
           9

"LET'S MAKE A RECYCLED SKELETON" LETTER

Dear Family,

We are studying the skeletal system in class. To help me learn the names of certain bones, you can show me how to make a "recycled skeleton" from pipe cleaners and bottle caps. Here are the directions.

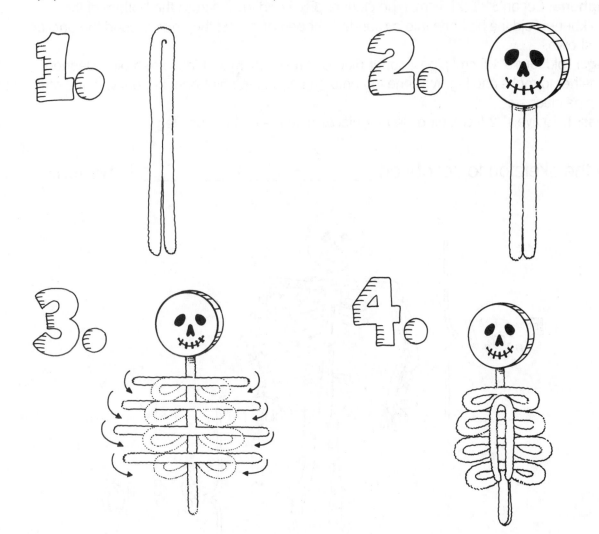

1. **Backbone:** Fold one pipe cleaner in half.
2. **Skull:** Sandwich one end of the backbone between two plastic bottle caps. Glue the caps together so the backbone stays inside. Draw eye sockets, a nose socket, and a mouth on the skull with black marker.
3. **Ribcage:** Cut one 6½" (16.5 cm), one 7" (17.5 cm), and two 8" (20.5 cm) pipe cleaner pieces. Lay the pieces across the backbone, as shown. Twist the pieces around the backbone so they stay in place. Fold the pipe cleaners forward and around to form ribs that meet in the center of the body.
4. **Breastbone:** Fold a 4" (10 cm) pipe cleaner piece in half and glue it where the ribs meet.

October © 1998 Creative Teaching Press

5. **Shoulder blades:** Twist a 6" (15 cm) pipe cleaner piece around the backbone along the top of the ribcage.
6. **Arms:** Fold four 6" (15 cm) pipe cleaner pieces in half. Link two of the folded pipe cleaners together to make one arm. Twist the arm onto one end of the shoulder blade. Repeat with the other set of pipe cleaners.
7. **Fingers:** Twist five 1" (2.5 cm) pipe cleaner pieces onto the end of each arm.
8. **Hipbone:** Cut an 8 ½" (21.5 cm) pipe cleaner piece and lay it across the bottom of the backbone. Fold the hipbone into a rounded shaped and twist the ends around the backbone as shown.
9. **Legs:** Fold four 6" (15 cm) pipe cleaner pieces in half. Link two of the folded pipe cleaners together to make one leg. Twist the leg onto one end of the hipbone. Repeat with the other set of pipe cleaners.
10. **Toes:** Twist five 1" (2.5 cm) pipe cleaner pieces onto the end of each leg.

Send the skeleton to school on _____. Have fun!

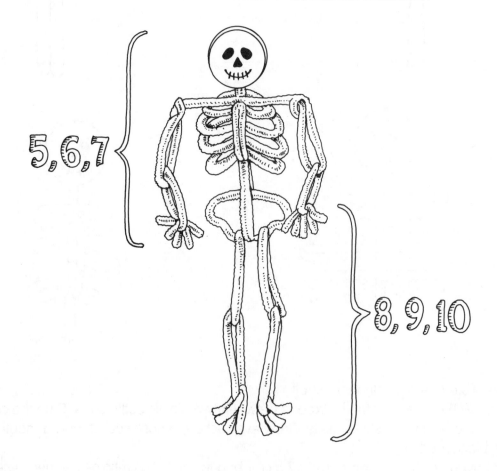

October © 1998 Creative Teaching Press

NATIONAL POPCORN MONTH

Keep your students popping with excitement by celebrating National Popcorn Month. October received this designation by the Popcorn Institute in celebration of popcorn as a wholesome, natural food. The following activities show why popcorn is so "pop"-ular!

LITERATURE LINKS

*Corn Is Maize:
The Gift of the Indians*
by Aliki

Popcorn
by Frank Asch

The Popcorn Book
by Tomie dePaola

The Popcorn Dragon
by Jane Thayer

Popcorn Magic
by Phyllis Adams, Carol P. Mitchner, and Virginia Johnson

"A Popcorn Song"
by Nancy Byrd Turner from
Sing a Song of Popcorn
selected by Beatrice Schenk deRegniers

Science Fun with Peanuts and Popcorn
by Rose Wyler

Riley

"POPCORN SCENES" BULLETIN BOARD

Brainstorm as a class real objects popcorn could be made to look like, such as snow, clouds, a white beard, or flowers. Then invite each student to draw on black construction paper a scene that incorporates popcorn. Ask students to color their scenes with crayon and glue on popcorn to fill in the scene. Display the scenes on a bulletin board titled *What Pops into Your Mind When You Hear "Popcorn"?*

MATERIALS
▲ black construction paper
▲ crayons
▲ popcorn
▲ glue

MATERIALS

▲ popcorn kernels
▲ resealable plastic bags
▲ tape
▲ chalkboard/chalk

COUNTING POPCORN

Place 20, 100, and 300 popcorn kernels in separate resealable plastic bags. Tape the bags to the chalkboard and invite students to guess which bag holds 100 kernels. Invite each student to make a tally mark under one of the bags to show his or her guess. Divide the class into three groups and have each group count the contents of a bag to find the answer. Then use the 100 kernels to complete the Flying Popcorn activity, below.

MATERIALS

▲ butcher paper
▲ air popper
▲ 100 popcorn kernels
▲ markers
▲ yardstick or meterstick

FLYING POPCORN

Place a long sheet of butcher paper on the floor. Place an air popper on the edge of the paper so the popper's "mouth" faces the length of the paper. Take the lid off the air popper and pop 100 popcorn kernels. As the kernels pop, fly, and land, invite students to mark an *X* to show their placement. Invite volunteers to measure how far the three farthest kernels flew. Write the distance next to each kernel. Draw a line where the air popper was and hang the butcher paper on the wall as a learning center. Invite students to measure the distance to the rest of the *X*s and write the measurements next to the marks.

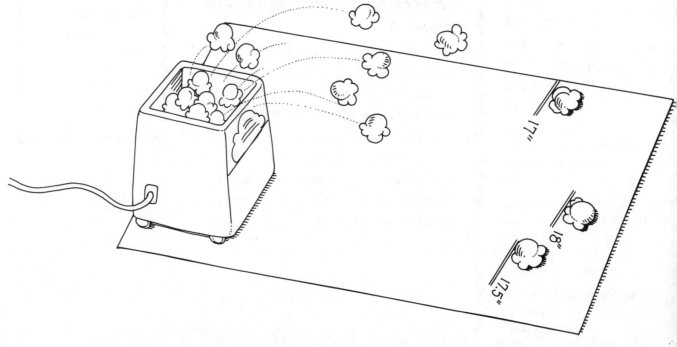

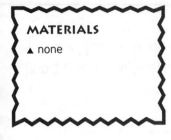

MATERIALS
▲ none

YUMMY SNACK SONG

Teach, and have students practice singing, the following popcorn song. Invite students to wear popcorn jewelry (below) and perform the song for families or other classes.

Yummy Snack Song
(to the tune of "Bingo")

There is a yummy snack I know
and popcorn is its name-o!
P-o-p-c-o-r-n, P-o-p-c-o-r-n, P-o-p-c-o-r-n,
and popcorn is its name-o!

MATERIALS
▲ popcorn and popcorn kernels
▲ sentence strips
▲ glue
▲ yarn
▲ large, dull craft needles

POPCORN JEWELRY

Invite students to make patterns with popcorn and popcorn kernels. Then have students glue the patterns onto sentence strips or string them onto yarn to make headbands, necklaces, and bracelets. Have students wear the jewelry when they perform "Yummy Snack Song" (above) or "The Popcorn Song" (page 34).

THE POPCORN SONG

Teach, and have students practice singing, the following popcorn song and accompanying motions. Invite students to wear "popcorn jewelry" (page 33) and perform the song for families or other classes.

The Popcorn Song	Motions
(to the tune of "Shortnin' Bread")	
We're going to make some nice warm popcorn. We're going to make some corn right now.	*Students jump up and down in place.*
Turn on the popper. Pour it in. Watch the kernels as they spin, spin, spin.	*Students turn on a "switch." Students pour. Students spin in place.*
Sprinkle some salt and Garlic or cheese. Choose a topping, if you please.	*Students make sprinkling motions.*
We're going to make some nice warm popcorn. We're going to make some corn right now.	*Students jump up and down in place.*

POPPING THROUGH THE SCIENTIFIC METHOD

Read the question on the Scientific Method reproducible and ask students to predict what will happen if they pop rainbow-colored popcorn kernels. Have students record their hypotheses on the reproducible. Pop rainbow-colored popcorn as a class. While the popcorn is popping, have students record the materials and procedure for the experiment. When the popcorn has popped, discuss, and have students record, the results. Then ask the class to come to conclusions about the results. (In most cases, the popcorn will *not* remain colored after it is popped. The corn turns out yellowish because the food coloring does not totally saturate the shell.) Have students record the results and conclusions before eating the popcorn.

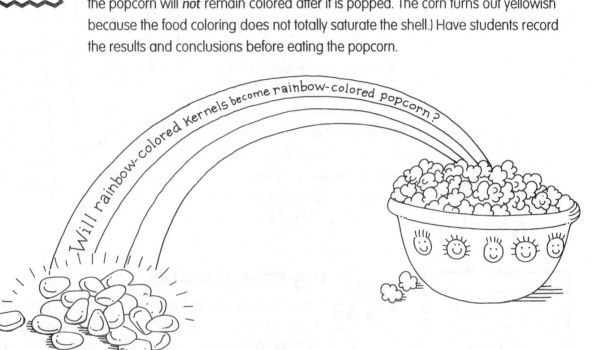

POPCORN GRAPH

Prepare three flavors of popcorn: buttered, cinnamon and sugar, and parmesan cheese. Invite students to taste each flavor. Ask students to choose their favorite, write their name on a white construction-paper cloud/popcorn shape, and tape the cloud to a butcher-paper graph labeled with each flavor. Compare the graphing results and discuss the favorite and least favorite flavors.

Buttered	Ray, Ricardo, Mary, Ana
Cinnamon and Sugar	Collin, Julia, Nick, Ruth, Tomas, Po, Chris
Parmesan Cheese	Maya, Sal, Vince, Travis

MATERIALS

▲ Popcorn Container reproducible (page 38)

▲ scissors

▲ crayons or markers

▲ tape

▲ Styrofoam packing peanuts

POPCORN MEMORIES

Invite each student to think of a special event during which he or she enjoyed popcorn, such as attending a movie, circus, birthday party, or baseball game. Invite students to write about their experience on a Popcorn Container reproducible. Have students color the container, cut it out, and tape it together. Ask students to fill the container with Styrofoam packing peanuts to represent popcorn. Display the containers in a reading center with the heading *Popcorn Memories.* Invite students to visit the center and read the stories.

MATERIALS

▲ wet paper towel

▲ clear plastic cups

▲ popcorn kernels

▲ sand

▲ blank book

PLANTING POPCORN

Invite each student to line a clear plastic cup with a wet paper towel. Have students place a handful of sand on the paper towel in the cup to hold the paper towel in place. Ask students to wedge four or five unpopped kernels along the sides of the cup between the cup and the paper towel. Invite students to take the cups home and observe the corn for growth over several days. Have students record their observations in a blank book (popcorn journal) and return the journal in seven to ten days. (Students and parents will be amazed at how quickly the corn grows!)

SCIENTIFIC METHOD

Question: Will rainbow-colored popcorn kernels become rainbow-colored popcorn?

Hypothesis: _____

_____

_____

Materials: _____

_____

_____

Procedure: _____

_____

_____

Results: _____

_____

_____

Conclusion: _____

_____

_____

POPCORN CONTAINER

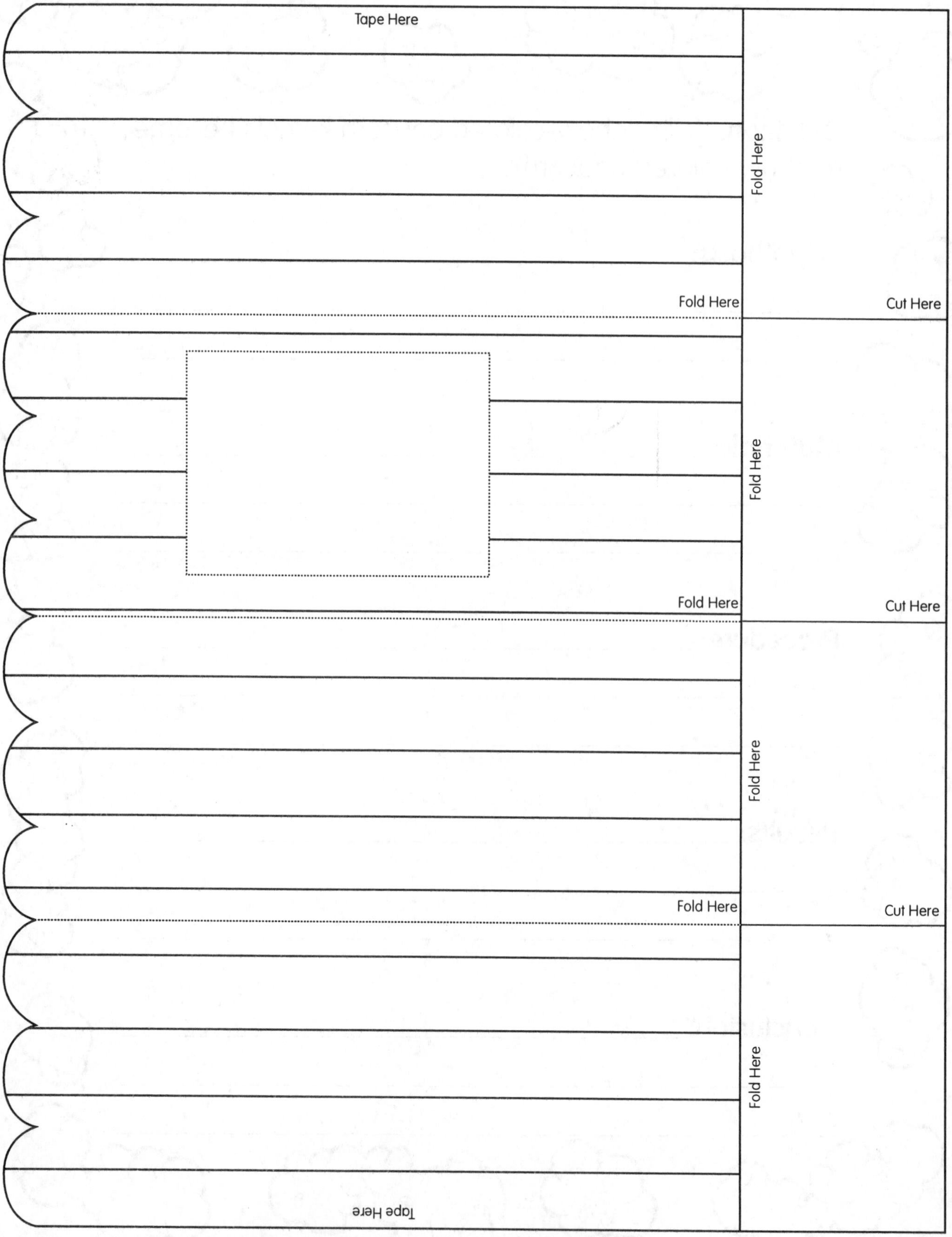

Tape Here

Fold Here

Fold Here

Cut Here

Fold Here

Fold Here

Cut Here

Fold Here

Fold Here

Cut Here

Fold Here

Tape Here

SPIDERS

Spiders—they're creepy, crawly, and oh so good for our environment! Invite your students to learn about and develop an appreciation for spiders by having them complete the following activities. Your students will soon be saying *Spiders are "spook-tacular"!*

LITERATURE LINKS

Anansi the Spider
by Gerald McDermott

Anansi and the Moss-Covered Rock
retold by Eric A. Kimmel

I Love Spiders
by John Parker

The Itsy Bitsy Spider
told and illustrated by Iza Trapani

The Spider Makes a Web
by Joan M. Lexau

Spiders
by Gail Gibbons

Spiders, Spiders Everywhere
by Rozanne Lanczak Williams (CTP)

The Very Busy Spider
by Eric Carle

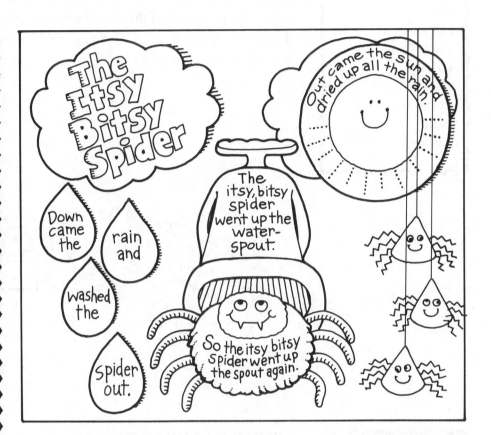

"ITSY BITSY SPIDER" BULLETIN BOARD

Cut from butcher paper a large black spider, two large white clouds, a light-blue waterspout, several light-blue raindrops, and a large yellow sun. Staple the cut-outs to a bulletin board to make the scene from "The Itsy Bitsy Spider." Write *The itsy bitsy spider went up the waterspout* on the waterspout, *Down came the rain and washed the spider out* on the raindrops, *Out came the sun and dried up all the rain* on the sun, and *So the itsy bitsy spider went up the spout again* on the spider. Have students make Hanging Spiders (page 40) and suspend them from the ceiling around the bulletin board.

MATERIALS

▲ black, white, light blue, and yellow butcher paper
▲ markers
▲ stapler
▲ Hanging Spiders (page 40)

HANGING SPIDERS

Invite each student to trace around a large margarine lid on black construction paper. Ask students to cut out the circle shape and then cut from one edge of the circle to the center to make a slit. Have students fold the circle into a cone shape and staple it in place. Invite students to accordion-fold eight black construction-paper strips and glue the strips on the underside of the cone. Ask students to glue on two wiggly eyes and draw a mouth with white crayon. String black yarn through the top of each cone and tape the yarn in place. Suspend the spiders around the Itsy Bitsy Spider Bulletin Board (page 39).

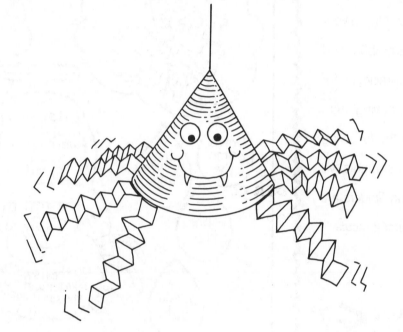

SPIDER HEADBANDS

Cut and staple black construction-paper strips to fit around each student's head (for headbands). Invite each student to stretch cotton balls into thin strips and glue them to the headband in X shapes to look like a spider web. Ask students to color and cut out a Spider Face reproducible and staple it to the center of the headband. Invite students to accordion-fold eight construction-paper strips and tape the strips to the top inside of the headband so they flop over the headband. Have students wear the headbands during spider activities such as There's a Spider on the . . . (page 41).

THERE'S A SPIDER ON THE . . .

Have students sing "There's a Spider on the Floor." Then ask students to think of new verses for the song such as *There's a spider on the desk, on the desk. There's a spider on the desk, on the desk. There's a spider on the desk, and he's making a big mess. There's a spider on the desk, on the desk.* Give students a hanging spider or spider headband to use as props as they sing and act out the new verses.

MATERIALS

▲ cassette or CD of "There's a Spider on the Floor" by Raffi (from *Singable Songs for the Very Young*)

▲ cassette or CD player

▲ Hanging Spiders (page 40) or Spider Headbands (page 40)

SPIDER CENTER

Set up a spider learning center in the classroom. Display several fiction and non-fiction spider books on a table. Surround the books with spider puppets and/or plastic, rubber, or stuffed spiders. Display spider photos and posters. Collect real spiders and place them in clear, well-ventilated containers for student observation. (Don't forget to feed them!) Place magnifying glasses and a large blank book (with one page for each student) on the table. Invite students to visit the center and explore. Ask each student to draw and write on a page of the blank book what he or she learned at the center.

MATERIALS

▲ fiction and nonfiction spider books (see Literature Links, page 39)

▲ spider puppets and/or plastic, rubber, or stuffed spiders

▲ spider photos and posters

▲ real spiders

▲ clear, well-ventilated containers

▲ magnifying glasses

▲ large blank book

▲ crayons or markers

SPIDERS COUNTING BOOK

Read aloud and discuss *Spiders, Spiders Everywhere.* Make a similar class book by first asking each student to choose a slip of paper that has a number written on it. Then ask each student to use a "bingo ink marker" to stamp that number of circles on a piece of construction paper. Have students add eight legs, a head, and clothing to each circle to make them into silly spiders similar to those in the book. Invite each student to write text on his or her page, such as *8 spiders on the bike.* Bind the pages in a class book titled *More Spiders Everywhere!*

SPIDER CREATIONS

Discuss spider body parts, such as the cephalothorax (head and chest combined), the abdomen, and the eight legs. Ask students to use a variety of art supplies to make an original spider that has each body part. Have the class vote and give an award to each spider for categories such as most realistic, most creative, most unusual, scariest, funniest, largest, smallest, or most interesting. Display the spiders on a table near the heading *What Do Spiders Have in Common?*

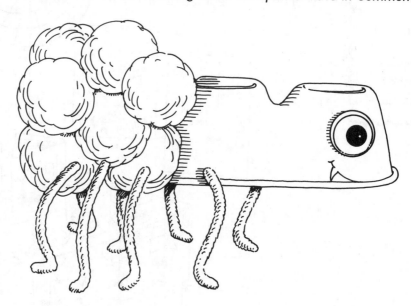

HANDY SPIDERS

MATERIALS

▲ paper plates
▲ black tempera paint
▲ 12" x 18" (30.5 cm x 46 cm) navy construction paper
▲ white crayon
▲ wiggly eyes
▲ glue
▲ insect stickers
▲ crayons or markers

Ask each student to use white crayon to draw a spider web in the center of navy construction paper. Pour black tempera paint into several paper plates. Invite each student to place his or her left hand in the paint and press it horizontally (so the fingers face left) in the center of the web. Then ask students to repeat the process with the right hand (the fingers should face right), overlapping the palm prints so the handprints look like a spider with eight legs. When the paint is dry, ask students to glue two wiggly eyes on the spider. Invite students to add one or two insect stickers to the web. Ask each student to write *I caught a/an (insect name) in my web* above the spider. Display the spiders for all to admire.

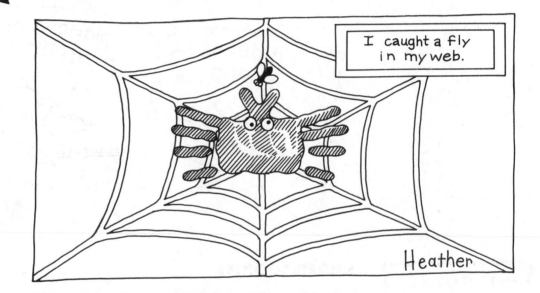

SENSATIONAL SPIDERS

MATERIALS

▲ large marshmallows
▲ mini M&Ms
▲ chow mein noodles
▲ chocolate syrup
▲ paper plates and napkins

Ask each student to push four chow mein noodles into each side of a large marshmallow to make a spider with eight legs. Have students squirt chocolate syrup over the marshmallow and place two mini M&Ms on the top for eyes. Invite students to sing "I Know an Old Lady Who Swallowed a Fly" and take a bite of the spider each time they reach the "spider part" in the song.

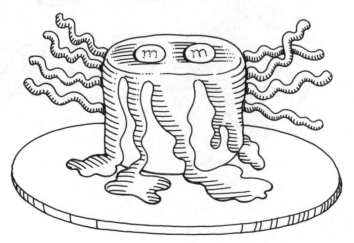

SPIDER SURPRISE BOOK

Students can surprise family members with this fun activity! Invite each student to fold a piece of white paper in half. Have students write *A spider is on my head* on the cover. Ask students to write *A spider is on my hand* on the inside left page. Instruct students to write *A spider is on my foot* on the inside right page. Have students write *A spider is on you!* on the back cover. Invite students to illustrate each page. Give each student a small plastic spider and his or her book to take home. Have students ask an "unsuspecting victim" to read the book. Students pull out the plastic spider and place it on the reader when he or she reads the last page. Invite students to share family members' reactions the next day—the kids love it!

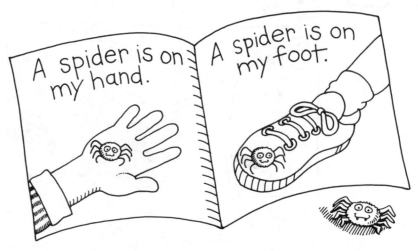

SPIDER COOKIES

Invite each student to frost two large sugar or oatmeal cookies. Then have students break four black licorice sticks in half and place four halves on each side of a cookie to make eight legs before they place the second cookie on top. Ask students to frost two M&Ms and place them on top for eyes. Invite students to eat their cookies while listening to a spider story.

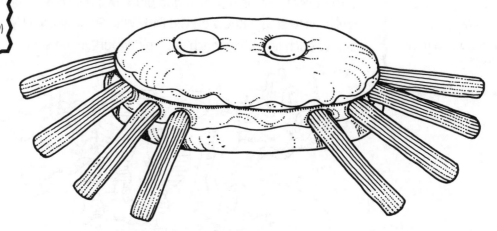

SPIDER STAMPS

Invite each student to cut seven slits in one end of a cardboard tube. Have students fold out the eight tube sections to a 90° angle to make "spider legs." Invite students to dip the spider legs into paint and press them onto construction paper to make a "spider" print. Ask students to dip a pencil eraser into paint and press it in the center of the prints twice to make spider eyes. Have students stretch cotton balls and glue them over the spiders to make a web. Display the spider stamps for all to admire.

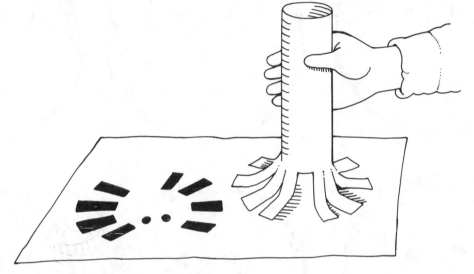

SPIDER WEBS

Read aloud and discuss *The Spider Makes a Web.* Then send home with each student a Spider Web letter, a large margarine lid, 2'–3' (61 cm to 91.5 cm) of white yarn, and a plastic spider. Ask students to follow the directions on the letter to make "spider webs" with their families and return the webs to school on a designated day. Invite students to share their experiences with web-making and tell if they think making a web is hard work for a spider.

SPIDER FACES

October © 1998 Creative Teaching Press

SPIDER WEB LETTER

Dear Family,

We are studying spiders at school, and one of the things we have learned is that spiders make webs! To help me learn about the hard work spiders do, please make a web with me following the directions below. We'll have a great time!

1. Cut out the center of a large margarine lid so only the ring remains.

2. Tie one end of the yarn to the ring. Tape or glue the yarn to the edge of the lid.

3. Loop the yarn tightly and evenly around the ring, as shown, until you return to the first loop.

4. Loop the yarn strand under and through the first set of loops to create a second row. (As you pull the string tightly, yarn "triangles" that stretch toward the ring's center will begin to form.)

5. Continue adding rows of loops moving toward the center of the ring.

6. When you reach the center of the web, knot the yarn, cut it off, and glue or tape it in place.

7. Glue a plastic spider to the center knot.

8. Send the completed web to school by _____.

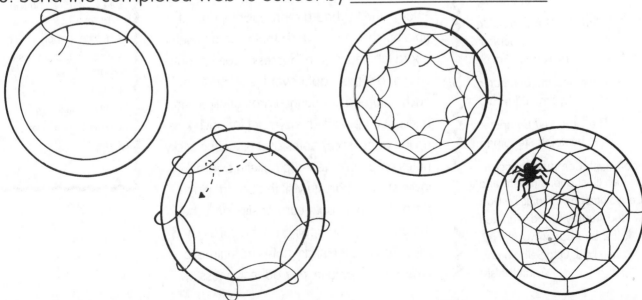

Spiders

COMPUTER LEARNING MONTH

Computers are everywhere and for everyone! And to increase computer literacy, October has been set aside as Computer Learning Month. Introduce your students to computers this October with the following activities—they're technologically terrific!

LITERATURE LINKS

The Brave Little Computer
by David Lyon

A Computer Went A-Courting
by Carol Greene

I Want to Be a Computer Operator
by Eugene Baker

Katie and the Computer
by Fred D'Ignzaio

The Little Red Computer
by Ralph Steadman

Books with Computer-generated Illustrations (*Bright and Early Thursday Evening* by Don and Audrey Wood, *The Red Racer* by Audrey Wood, *Free Lunch* by J. Otto Seibold and Vivian Walsh)

"KEYBOARD FLIP-UP" BULLETIN BOARD

Enlarge the Keyboard reproducible, trace it onto butcher paper, and staple it to a bulletin board labeled *Keys to Success.* Tape an index card or a slip of paper over the symbol on each enlarged key so the cards or slips can be flipped up. Write the symbol for each key on individual sticky notes and place the sticky notes on a table near the bulletin board. Invite student pairs to visit the board, place each sticky note on a card or slip, and check the placement by flipping up the cards or slips. Replace the sticky notes from time to time when they lose their adhesiveness.

MATERIALS
▲ Keyboard reproducible (page 51)
▲ butcher paper
▲ index cards or slips of paper
▲ tape
▲ sticky notes
▲ crayons or markers
▲ stapler

MATERIALS

▲ computer
▲ six sticky notes
▲ markers
▲ clock with a second hand

HARDWARE RACE

Point out the monitor, printer, keyboard, disk drive, mouse, and modem on a classroom computer. Write the word for each part on a different sticky note. Divide the class into groups of six. Give each member of one group a sticky note turned facedown. Invite members of the "note group" to run a relay (from a designated starting point to the computer) in which they place the sticky note on the computer in the correct spot before returning to the starting line. Time the relay and note how long the group took to finish. Repeat the relay with each group. The group with the shortest time wins.

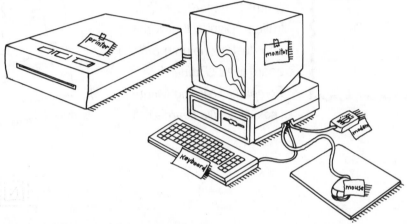

MATERIALS

▲ I.P.O. Slips (page 52)
▲ scissors
▲ container

INPUT, PROCESSING, OUTPUT

Photocopy and cut apart the I.P.O. slips and place them in a container. (Keep the original reproducible as an answer key.) Explain how computers operate—information is entered into a computer through a keyboard, mouse, scanner, or joystick (input); the computer uses its "brain", the Central Processing Unit (CPU) and its memory to make changes, calculate equations, check spelling, or perform other functions (processing); and the computer shows the processed information to the user through a printer, a video monitor, or audio speakers (output). Write *Input, Processing,* and *Output* on the chalkboard. Invite a student to take an I.P.O. slip from the jar and help him or her read it. Ask the student to take a guess and stand under *Input, Processing,* or *Output* to show what kind of computer operation the slip is describing. Continue the game with other volunteers and I.P.O. slips until all the slips are gone.

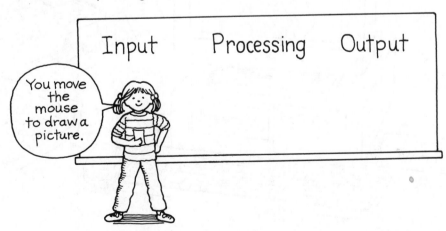

COMPUTER DESIGNERS

Share several books with computer-generated illustrations. Then invite each student to write an October-theme story and generate a computer drawing to go with it. Have students use computer programs to generate their illustrations. Display the stories and illustrations on a bulletin board titled *October Is Computer Learning Month. Look What We Learned!*

COMPUTER INTERVIEW

Invite each student to take home an Interview reproducible and interview an adult whose job requires him or her to use a computer. Remind students that most cash registers, price scanners, and receipt generators (from gas stations, delivery services, etc.) are computers. Have six or seven students return and share their interview results each week throughout the month of October.

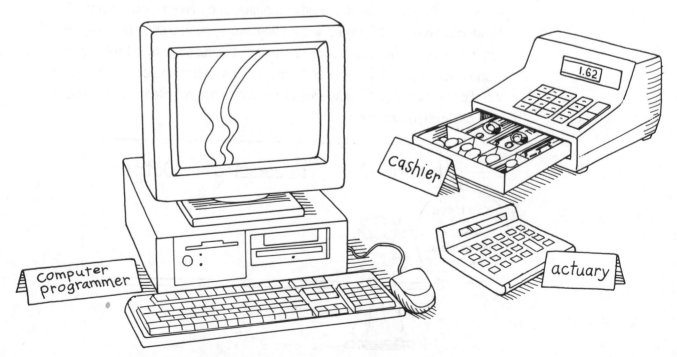

KEYBOARD

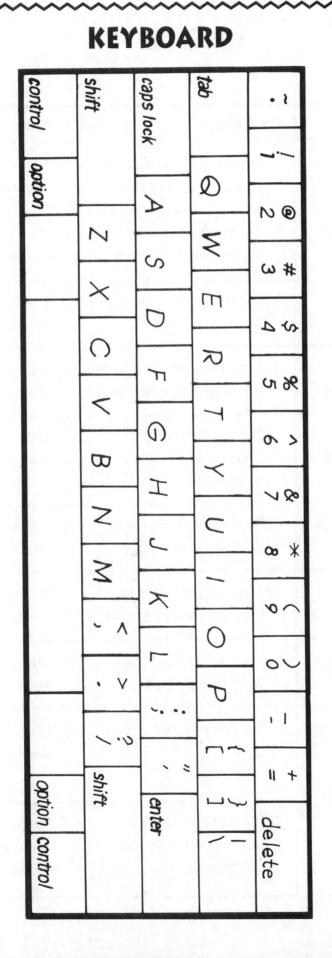

I.P.O. SLIPS

Input	Processing	Output
1. You use the keyboard to type a story.	1. The computer corrects all your spelling mistakes.	1. The printer prints out a story you typed.
2. You move the mouse to draw a picture.	2. The computer switches the order of two letters.	2. The printer prints out a picture.
3. You use a scanner to scan a photo.	3. The computer multiplies 2 X 2.	3. The monitor shows the answer to a math question.
4. You use the joystick to "knock down a building."	4. The computer tells you the meaning of the word *echo.*	4. You hear a beep when you make a mistake.
5. You use the number keys to type a math problem.	5. The computer changes a lowercase letter into a capital letter.	5. The speakers play a song from a CD-ROM game.
6. You push the escape key to leave a program.	6. The computer moves a word to the next line.	6. The monitor shows a bar graph.
7. You double-click on the mouse to choose a picture.	7. The computer skips two lines between sentences.	7. The monitor shows an e-mail from your friend.
8. You push the return key to go to a new line.	8. The computer numbers your math problems.	8. The speakers show you what a tiger sounds like.
9. You push the "Caps Lock" key to make all capital letters.	9. The computer saves your work.	9. The printer prints out your math homework.
10. You type in your code name to go on-line.	10. The computer dials a phone number so you can go on-line.	10. The speakers chime when you get a correct answer in a video game.

October © 1998 Creative Teaching Press

Name_____

INTERVIEW

1. What is your name and job description?

_____

_____

2. How do you use computers at work?

_____

_____

3. Did you need special training to learn to use a computer? _____
   If so, what kind?

_____

_____

4. Is your job easier because of computers? _____ How? _____

_____

_____

5. What did people with your job do before computers existed?

_____

_____

OKTOBERFEST

Oktoberfest is a German festival held in Munich each autumn. Oktoberfest began in the 1800s after a royal wedding. During the festival, German people meet in large banquet halls to enjoy traditional German food, drink, and music.

LITERATURE LINKS

Germany
by Richard Lord

The Land and People of Germany
by Raymond Wohlrabe and Werner E. Krusch

Munich
by Lilia Schacherel

Oktoberfest in Munich (videotape and cassette)
by Landmark Films, Barinder Productions, 1987

This Is Munich
by Miroslav Sasek

"OKTOBERFEST-IVAL OF FAIRY TALES" BULLETIN BOARD

Explain that Oktoberfest is a traditional German celebration and that the Brothers Grimm (Jakob and Wilhelm) are two of Germany's most famous children's authors. Invite the class to use art supplies to create an Oktoberfest bulletin board scene (without people) that includes a bandstand, an Oktoberfest hall, and carnival rides such as a ferris wheel. Label the bulletin board *Oktoberfest-ival of Fairy Tales!* Read aloud several Grimms' fairy tales. Ask each student to draw, color, and cut out a character from one of the fairy tales and staple the character to the bulletin board.

MATERIALS
▲ butcher paper
▲ art supplies (construction paper, crayons or markers, tempera paint/paintbrushes, scissors, glue)
▲ Grimms' fairy tales (such as *The Bremen Town Musicians, The Elves and the Shoemaker, The Golden Goose, Hansel and Gretel, Snow White, Rapunzel, Rumpilstiltskin,* and *Tom Thumb*)

MUSICFEST

Explain that music is an important part of the Oktoberfest celebration. Play music by a classical German composer such as Brahms, Beethoven, or Bach, and invite students to use kazoos to play along. If possible, play some traditional German "oompah-band" music and have students play along with one of those songs as well.

MATERIALS

cassette or CD player

cassette or CD of music by a classical German composer (such as Brahms, Beethoven, or Bach)

cassette or CD of music by a traditional German "oompah band"

kazoos

YOUR OWN OKTOBERFEST

Set up your own Oktoberfest in the classroom. Invite each student to glue together horizontally a black, a red, and a yellow construction-paper strip to make the stripes on a German flag. String the flags onto yarn and hang the yarn across the classroom. Have students decorate and wear sentence-strip lederhosen suspenders that are hole-punched on the ends and attached to belt loops by string. (Students without belt loops can tape them to their clothing.) Then serve German food samples such as sauerkraut, bratwurst, dark rye bread, pretzels, apple strudel, and root beer to make the party complete.

MATERIALS

- black, red, and yellow construction paper
- crayons or markers
- sentence strips
- tape
- hole punch
- string
- German food samples (sauerkraut, bratwurst, dark rye bread, pretzels, apple strudel, root beer)
- paper plates, napkins, plastic forks, and cups

SCARECROW DAY

A not-so-scary symbol for October is the scarecrow. A scarecrow is a hay-stuffed mannequin placed in farmers' fields to scare crows and other birds away from crops. Invite your students to have some fun with the following scarecrow activities. They'll be crowing about it through October and the rest of the year!

LITERATURE LINKS

Hello, Mr. Scarecrow
by Rob Lewis

The Scarebird
by Sid Fleischman

Scarecrow
by Valerie LIttlewood

Scarecrows
by Robert Westall

Scarecrow's Secret
by H. Amery

Don't Be Scared of Compound Words!

"DON'T BE SCARED" BULLETIN BOARD

Review and practice compound words with this fun activity. Explain the meaning of a compound word, using the word *scarecrow* as an example. Make a class list of compound words and invite each student to choose his or her favorite. Invite students to color and cut out a scarecrow reproducible. Have each student write his or her compound word in the center of the scarecrow. Ask students to fold the scarecrow's arms on the dotted lines and color the other side of the arms to match the already-colored clothing. Have students use black crayon to write the first half of the compound word on the left arm and the second half of the word on the right arm. Display the scarecrows on a bulletin board titled *Don't Be Scared of Compound Words!*

MATERIALS
▲ Scarecrow repro-
   ducible (page 59)
▲ crayons
▲ scissors

MATERIALS

▲ two broomsticks or mop handles

▲ hammer/nails

▲ large paper grocery sack

▲ newspaper

▲ crayons or markers

▲ rope

▲ shirt, pants, gloves, shoes

▲ hay

▲ white construction paper

▲ laminator

▲ dry-erase markers

CLASSROOM SCARECROW

Nail two broomsticks or mop handles together to make a *T*, and then make a scarecrow together as a class. Divide the class into four groups. Have one group fill a large paper grocery sack with newspaper, decorate a face with crayons or markers, place the sack over the top of the *T*, and tie the head in place with a rope. Ask another group to stuff a shirt with hay and place it on the arms of the *T*. Invite another group to stuff pants with hay and put one leg on the base of the *T*. Have another group stuff gloves, shoes, and a hat and add them to the scarecrow. Lean the scarecrow in a corner of the classroom. Tape a laminated white construction-paper speech bubble just above the scarecrow's head. The next morning, before students arrive, write a message on the speech bubble, such as *Today we have music class*. Invite students to read the message as they enter. Keep the scarecrow in the room throughout October and change the message each morning.

SCARE WHOM? CLASS BOOK

Invite each student to think of one real or imaginary thing he or she would like to scare away, such as bad dreams or space creatures. Have students draw on construction paper a scarecrow with special features designed to scare away the thing they chose. Ask students to name the scarecrow and write its name above the drawing. Bind the pages in a class book titled *Scare Whom?*

MATERIALS

▲ construction paper

▲ crayons or markers

▲ bookbinding materials

SCARECROW FLIP-UP BOOKS

Have each student fold and cut into fourths a piece of white paper. Ask students to staple the four pieces together at the top to make a flip-up book. Have students write the following sentence frame on each of the squares: *You scared the _____ bird.* Ask students to fill each blank with a different color word. Invite students to staple the flip-up book in the center of a Flip-Up Book reproducible. Show the class how to read their books: They read the left side of the reproducible, a center flip-up page, and the right side of the reproducible. Have students illustrate their flip-up pages, color the reproducible, and read the book to a partner.

SCARECROW WORDS BULLETIN BOARD

Invite each student to decorate a paper plate with button eyes, a construction-paper triangle nose, and a yarn mouth. Have students glue straw around the bottom of the plate. Ask each student to design a construction paper "scarecrow hat" to glue on top. Invite each student to think of a scarecrow-related word (such as *crow, garden, straw, fence,* or *corn)* and write it in large print on the hat. Staple the scarecrow faces to a bulletin board titled *We're Crowing about Scarecrows!* Have students refer to the words as they write stories throughout the month of October.

SCARECROW

FLIP-UP BOOK

October © 1998 Creative Teaching Press

COLUMBUS DAY

Italian explorer Christopher Columbus set sail from Spain on August 3, 1492, to find a route to the Indies. Instead, he found Central, South, and North America. Columbus Day commemorates Columbus' voyages to the "new world." Help your students become explorers of history with the following Columbus Day activities—they'll make a lot of "discoveries"!

LITERATURE LINKS

Christopher Columbus
by Rae Bains

Christopher Columbus: A Great Explorer
by Carol Greene

The Great Adventure of Christopher Columbus
by Jean Fritz

I, Christopher Columbus
by Lisa Weil

In 1492
by Jean Marzollo

Learning to Follow Directions with Columbus!

Niña   Pinta   Santa Maria

Joseph

"FOLLOWING DIRECTIONS" SHIPS

Use this activity to help students learn to follow directions. Ask each student to round the corners of three white paper squares to form circles. Have students cut each circle in half and use three of the halves to form the three ships of Columbus. Ask students to cut the leftover halves in half (quarters) to create two sails for each ship. Invite students to draw the ocean on the bottom half of a piece of light-blue construction paper. Have students glue the circle halves (ship bottoms) on the ocean. Invite students to draw a mast for each ship and then glue on the sails as shown. Invite students to add details with crayons. Display the pictures on a bulletin board titled *Learning to Follow Directions with Columbus!*

MATERIALS
- ▲ 4" (10 cm) white construction paper squares
- ▲ 12" x 18" (30.5 cm x 46 cm) light-blue construction paper
- ▲ construction paper scraps
- ▲ crayons or markers
- ▲ scissors
- ▲ glue

PERSONAL DISCOVERIES

Discuss Columbus' quest to make a new discovery and the hard work he put into achieving his goals. Ask each student to think of a personal "discovery" he or she would like to make, such as how to ride a bike or a way to get an *A* on every spelling test. Invite each student to follow the directions on the Ship Bottom reproducible and write about his or her quest. Then invite students to follow the directions on the Ship Sail reproducible to make a completed ship. Display the ships on a table labeled *In Search of Our Own New World!*

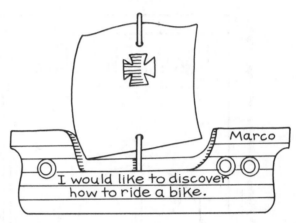

WIND POWER

Discuss how Columbus traveled to the "new world" in ships powered by wind. Then invite students to have a race to study the effects of wind power. Invite each student to place a dime-size ball of modeling clay in the bottom of a walnut shell half as a ship bottom. Have students design a paper sail and tape it to a tooth-pick. Have students push the toothpicks into the clay in their shell. Place a tub of water on a table. Write *Spain* on one side of the tub and *The New World* on the other. One at a time, have students blow their ship from "Spain" to "The New World" as you time each "trip."

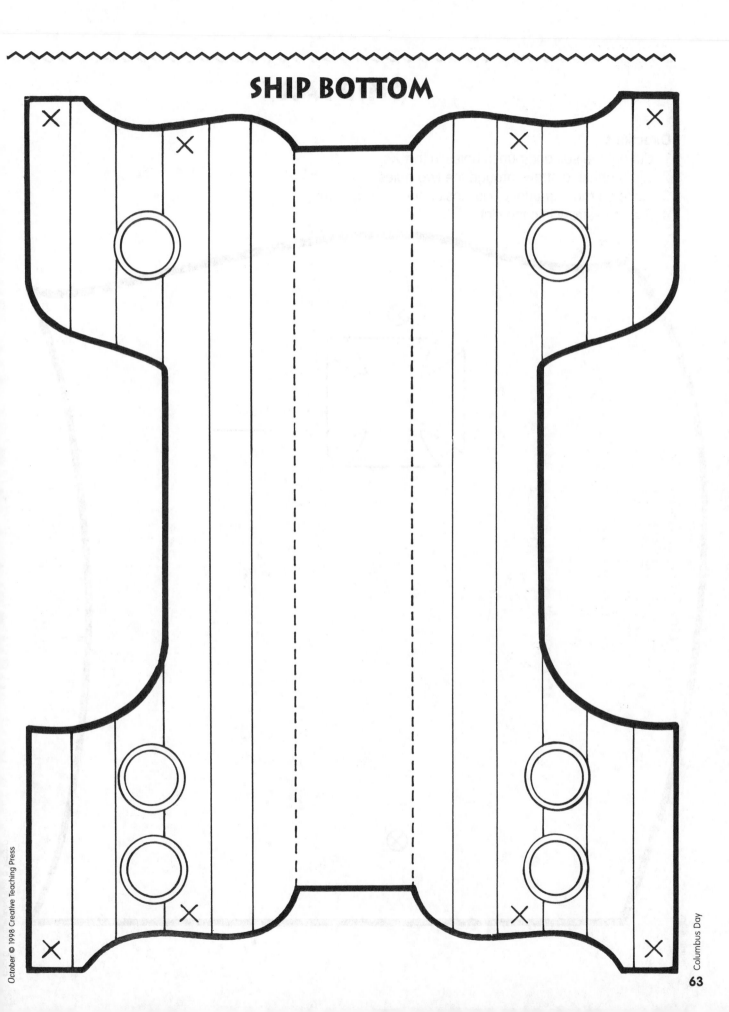

SHIP BOTTOM

SHIP SAIL

Directions:
1. Cut out the sail and punch holes in the Xs.
2. Slip a drinking straw through the two holes.
3. Place a small amount of clay inside the "ship bottom."
4. Push the straw into the clay.

October © 1998 Creative Teaching Press

GOOD SPELLING DAY

October 16

October 16 marks the birthday of Noah Webster, the famous educator who created a spelling book for his students that became *An American Dictionary of the English Language.* Webster's work helped standardize English spelling and pronunciation and has become one of the most-read books in the world.

LITERATURE LINKS

The Cat in the Hat Beginner Book Dictionary
by P.D. Eastman

Longman Picture Wordbook
by Brian Abbs

A Magic World of Words
edited by William D. Halsey
and Christopher G. Morris

My First Dictionary
by Stephen Krensky

The Spelling Bee
by Sharon Gordon

OCTOBER CLASS DICTIONARY

Have each student use tempera paint and a letter sponge to stamp a different letter on construction paper. Invite students to think of an October word (or group of words) for their letter, such as *apple* for *A, bale of hay* for *B,* and *cider* for *C.* Help students write the word(s) under the stamp on the construction paper. Ask students to illustrate their chosen word(s). Bind the pages into a class book. For the rest of October, feature one or two book-page words on each week's spelling list. Challenge students to study the words and spell them correctly on the test at the end of the week.

MATERIALS
- ▲ tempera paint
- ▲ letter sponges
- ▲ white construction paper
- ▲ crayons or markers
- ▲ bookbinding materials

OCTOBER CHALLENGE WORDS

Reproduce the Challenge Words reproducible, cut apart the word cards, and give a word to each student. Invite students to take the word home, learn how spell it, discover what it means, and return the word by a designated day. On the return day, divide the class into groups. Invite a student to stand in front of the class and read and spell his or her word. Have groups meet and discuss the meaning of the recited word. Invite the "word reader" to choose a volunteer from each group, listen to his or her predictions, and reveal the word's meaning. Continue the game until each student has had a chance to read and spell his or her word.

DICTIONARY RACE

Divide the class into pairs. Choose a word from the Challenge Words reproducible and read it aloud. (Do not show the word. If you have to, tell students the first letter.) Invite pairs to find the word in the dictionary as quickly as possible and raise their hands. Ask the first pair who found the word to spell it and award that pair a point. Have a race with each challenge word and have pairs tally their points to determine a winner.

CHALLENGE WORDS

October	spider	scarecrow
ghost	jack-o'-lantern	masquerade
skeleton	treat	pumpkin
harvest	autumn	gourd
haunt	spook	wizard
goblin	shiver	leaves
jacket	sweater	chilly
magic	frighten	trick
treat	costume	orange
bat	cider	howl

PAUL BUNYAN DAY

Paul Bunyan, the legendary lumberjack, is a favorite character in traditional American tall tales. And October, with its windy days and chilly nights, is the perfect time to read about Paul and his adventures in the North Woods. Introduce your students to Paul Bunyan with the following activities—they're larger than life!

LITERATURE LINKS

Paul Bunyan
retold by Ellen M. Dolan and Janet L. Bolinske

Paul Bunyan
by Brian Gleeson

Paul Bunyan
by Steven Kellogg

Paul Bunyan & Babe the Blue Ox
by Jan Gleiter and Kathleen Thompson

Paul Bunyan Swings His Ax
by Dell J. McCormick

"Sky-Bright Ax/Paul Bunyan"
from *American Tall Tales*
by Adrien Stoutenberg

This is Pat. Once Pat and Paul cut down the Jolly Green Giant's stalk.

LOOK LIKE A LUMBERJACK

The night before Paul Bunyan Day, send home a note inviting students to come to school the next day dressed like Paul Bunyan. Offer clothing suggestions such as plaid flannel shirts, blue jeans, boots, tasseled hats, and any other "lumberjack" apparel they can imagine. Take a Polaroid photo of each "lumberjack" and glue each photo to a piece of construction paper. Read aloud several Paul Bunyan stories. Have students think up a far-fetched adventure they could have with Paul Bunyan. Instruct students to write the following sentence frames under the photo to share their adventure idea: *This is (student name). Once (student name) and Paul (adventure idea).* Invite students to share their adventure idea and then bind the pages in a class book titled *Paul Bunyan's Friends.*

MATERIALS
▲ note to parents
▲ student "lumberjack clothing"
▲ Paul Bunyan stories (see Literature Links)
▲ Polaroid camera/film
▲ construction paper
▲ crayons or markers
▲ bookbinding materials

GIANT GRIDDLES

Read aloud a Paul Bunyan story that includes the tale of the giant pancake griddle and men skating on bacon to keep the griddle greased. Then have each student design his or her own "giant griddle." Invite each student to decorate a paper plate to look like the inside of a griddle. Have students draw butter on the griddle. Invite students to cut out and attach construction-paper "ice skating" lumberjacks. Ask each student to design and tape a cardboard-tube griddle handle to the paper plate. Staple the griddles to a bulletin board titled *Pancake Makin' with Strips of Bacon!*

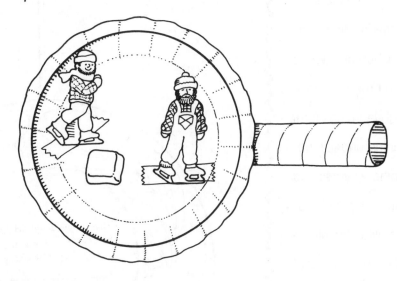

POPCORN BLIZZARD

Read aloud a Paul Bunyan story that includes the tale of the "popcorn blizzard." Then invite students to draw on construction paper a scene from the tale and glue on pieces of popcorn to complete their scene. Ask students to write a short description under the picture. Display the blizzard scenes near the heading *Paul and the Popcorn Blizzard.*

The sun was so hot that the corn popped and made a popcorn blizzard!

UNITED NATIONS DAY

October 24

The United Nations was established after World War II to promote peace through learning about and gaining understanding of other cultures and countries. Help your students complete the following activities to learn about the UN and its work.

LITERATURE LINKS

The Big Book for Peace
edited by Ann Durell and
Marilyn Sachs

Children As Teachers of Peace
by Gerald G. Jampolsky

A Country Far Away
by Nigel Gray

This Is the United Nations
by M. Sasek

United Nations:
A New True Book
by Carol Green

This is how I would help the people of the world live together peacefully:

I would give a job to all adults.

"OLIVE BRANCH" HANGERS

Explain that the olive branch, a symbol of peace, appears on the flag of the United Nations. Invite students to imagine they are ambassadors to the UN and share one way they would help the people of the world live together peacefully. Have students write their idea in the center of an "Olive Branch" Hanger. Ask students to color the hanger, cut it out, and decorate the other side to illustrate their ideas. Invite students to punch a hole in the hanger top, tie yarn through the hole, and hang their olive branches from the ceiling.

MATERIALS
▲ "Olive Branch" Hanger (page 72)
▲ crayons or markers
▲ scissors
▲ hole punch
▲ yarn

HERITAGE FESTIVAL OF FOOD

Point out on a world map several countries that belong to the United Nations. Invite students to go home and find out the name of one country from which their ancestors came. Ask students to prepare a traditional food that came from that country and bring it to school on United Nations Day. Have each student share the name of the food he or she brought and the country from which it came. Then invite the class to "dig in"!

"HELP A NATION" PLAN

Explain that the UN helps underdeveloped nations bring much-needed supplies and education to their citizens. For example, assistance is offered in food production and distribution and schools are established and staffed. Have student groups imagine they are the head of the UN Development Program, the division in charge of helping other nations. Ask groups to develop a list of ways to help an imaginary nation called *Newland.* Explain that Newland has no farms, schools, paved roads, or hospitals. Invite groups to prioritize their list from most important to least important as a way to determine what they would do first to help the nation. Have groups read their lists and share what they would do and why.

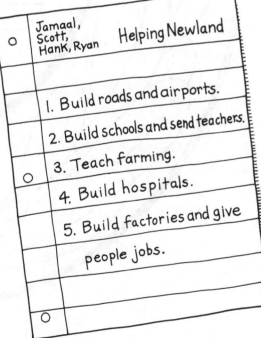

Jamaal, Scott, Hank, Ryan   Helping Newland

1. Build roads and airports.

2. Build schools and send teachers.

3. Teach farming.

4. Build hospitals.

5. Build factories and give people jobs.

"OLIVE BRANCH" HANGER

This is how I would help the people of the world live together peacefully:

_____

_____

_____

_____

October © 1998 Creative Teaching Press

PICASSO DAY

Darcy

October 25

Pablo Picasso began painting at the age of 14. He experimented with realistic painting, but he is best known for Cubism, a style in which objects resemble three-dimensional geometric shapes. Your students can learn more about Picasso with the following activities that will add a new "dimension" to their learning!

LITERATURE LINKS

Getting to Know the World's Greatest Artists: Picasso by Mike Venezia

Pablo Picasso by Ernest Raboff

Pablo Picasso: The Minotaur by Daniele Giraudy

Picasso by Ibi Lepscky

Shapes by Philip Yenawine

THREE-DIMENSIONAL ART

Read aloud *Getting to Know the World's Greatest Artists: Picasso.* Discuss how Picasso was a master at painting objects on a flat piece of paper so they looked three-dimensional (having width, length, and depth). Display several 3-D geometric shapes, such as a cylinder, pyramid, or cube. Invite students to compare the shapes to real classroom objects of the same shape. Invite students to draw 3-D shapes on white construction paper and turn them into objects such as faces, buildings, or instruments. Display the illustrations on a bulletin board titled *3-D Fun!*

MATERIALS
▲ *Getting to Know the World's Greatest Artists: Picasso* by Mike Venezia
▲ classroom objects
▲ white construction paper
▲ crayons or markers

"BLUE PERIOD" ART

Share photographs of Picasso's paintings from his *Blue Period.* Then invite students to make their own blue paintings. Have students sketch a still-life scene displayed on a table. Ask students to mix blue, white, and black tempera paints in an egg carton to create several shades of blue. Invite students to use construction paper and the shades they created to paint their sketch. Display the paintings near the heading *Painting Blue Like Picasso!*

CUBISM CUBE

Tape shut a small square cardboard box so the lid stays in place. Write a phrase related to Picasso on each side of the box: *his paintings, his childhood, his life as an artist, his cartoons, his drawings, his use of color and geometry.* Read aloud and discuss several books about Picasso. Have the class sit in a circle. Toss the box to a student. Have the student read the phrase that appears on the side of the box that is facing up. Invite that student to share one "Picasso fact" related to the phrase. (The student can call on friends to help if he or she cannot remember a fact.) Ask that student to toss the box to another student to continue the game. Have students toss the cube until each student has had a turn.

TEDDY BEAR DAY

October 27

Theodore Roosevelt was born on October 27. According to legend, Roosevelt protected from hunters a bear cub who wandered into his campsite. A newspaper printed a cartoon of the scene that inspired the making of the first "teddy bear." Invite your students to celebrate Teddy's birthday with the following "beary" fun activities.

LITERATURE LINKS

Bears, Bears Everywhere
by Luella Connelly (CTP)

Corduroy
by Don Freeman

How Teddy Bears Are Made
by Ann Morris

The One Bad Thing about Father
by F. N. Monjo (a story about Theodore Roosevelt)

Teddy Bear's Picnic
by Jimmy Kennedy

Wish Again, Big Bear
by Richard Margolis

TEDDY BEAR COSTUMES

Invite each student to bring a teddy bear or other stuffed animal to school. Have students use costume-making supplies to design a costume for their stuffed animal. Line up the animals along the floor to make a "costume parade." Invite students to vote for costume awards in categories such as funniest, scariest, most realistic, best use of materials, or most unusual. Be sure each costume receives an award.

MATERIALS
- ▲ teddy bears or stuffed animals brought from home
- ▲ costume-making supplies (fabric scraps, felt, yarn, wallpaper scraps, dime-store masks, pipe cleaners, buttons, ribbon, construction paper, scissors, fabric glue, tape, hole punch)

TEDDY BEARS AT NIGHT

MATERIALS

▲ *Corduroy* by Don Freeman

▲ teddy bears or stuffed animals brought from home

▲ writing paper

Invite each student to bring a teddy bear or other stuffed animal to school. Have students (and their bears) listen as you read *Corduroy*. Invite students to leave their bears at school overnight, and ask students *What do you think your stuffed animals do at night?* After students leave for the day, position the bears so they look like they have had some fun. Arrange the bears with books in the reading corner, with games on the carpet, and with math manipulatives at desks. Hang bears from the lights, hide some inside desks and bookshelves, and place one or two in your chair. When students arrive the next morning, they will be shocked and delighted! Invite students to use the scene as inspiration for a story called *Teddy Bears at Night*.

TEDDY BEAR MATH

MATERIALS

▲ teddy bears or stuffed animals brought from home

▲ rulers

▲ sentence strips

▲ crayons or markers

▲ scissors

▲ tape

Invite each student to bring a teddy bear or other stuffed animal to school. Have students sit with their animals in a circle. Have the class sort the animals by size, color, shape, "species," and clothing. Invite the class to make several patterns with the animals. Have students place the animals in line from smallest to largest. Ask each student to use a ruler and measure the height or length of his or her animal. Then invite students to use a sentence strip to measure the circumference of their animal's head. Have students cut and tape the sentence strip to fit the animal's head and decorate it as a crown. "Invite" the animals to wear the crowns for the rest of the day.

MARVELOUS MASKS DAY

All over the world, October is celebrated with festivals and masquerade balls at which people wear masks. Your students can wear masks, too, when you help them complete one of the following activities. They won't be able to "mask" their excitement!

LITERATURE LINKS

The Big Book of Animal Masks
by Angela Holroyd

Makeup & Masks
by Ellen Terry and Lynne Anderson

Making Masks & Crazy Faces
by Jen Green

Masks & Funny Faces
by Denny Robson

Play Mask Book
by Kate Davies

GOOFY GLASSES MASKS

Invite each student to bring to school a pair of old sunglasses without the lenses. Have students use art supplies to add features to the glasses to make them into masks. Students can add paper noses or beaks, eyelashes from paper with slits, paper ears that are connected to the glasses temples, or false foreheads that are taped or glued above the lenses. Encourage students to use their imagination when designing mask features. When the masks are complete, hold a goofy glasses parade and invite your students to show off their designs.

MATERIALS
▲ old sunglasses
▲ art supplies (construction paper, pipe cleaners, feathers, buttons, crayons or markers, paint/paintbrushes)
▲ tape
▲ glue
▲ scissors

NATURE MASKS

Invite each student to brush glue on a dime-store mask to cover it. Have students carefully place real or plastic leaves in a pattern on the mask (so the leaf ends point out). Have students wrap leaves around and through the eye holes so the holes are not completely covered. Have student groups create short skits in which they pretend to be trees with falling October leaves. Invite students to wear their masks as their group performs the skit.

MOOD MASKS

Explain that for thousands of years people have been wearing masks in plays to show characters' moods. Invite each student to choose two opposing emotions such as happy/sad, cowardly/brave, angry/content, or busy/bored. Ask students to paint on a paper plate faces that show both emotions, one emotion on each side of the plate. Ask students to tape a craft stick or tongue depressor onto the bottom of the plate. Invite each student to hold up the mask in front of his or her face and turn it so the class can see both sides. Invite the class to guess the emotions displayed.

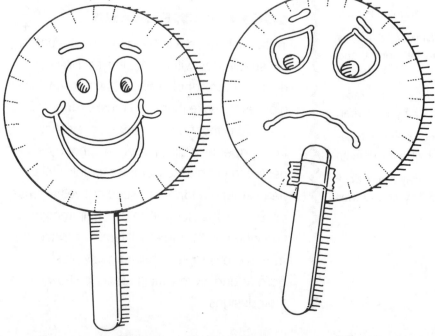

CRAZY CLOCK DAY

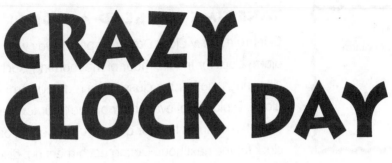

October is National Clock Month and marks the end of Daylight Savings Time. Invite your students to celebrate the clock as a great invention with the following Crazy Clock Day activities—they'll have the "time" of their lives!

LITERATURE LINKS

Around the Clock with Harriet
by Betsy Maestro

A Clock for Beany
by Lisa Bassett

Clocks and How They Go
by Gail Gibbons

Clocks and More Clocks
by Pat Hutchins

Tick-Tock Clock
by Sharon Gordon

by Conan

"TRULY CUCKOO" CLOCKS

Invite each student to trace around a small margarine lid on construction paper and cut out the circle. Ask students to draw a clock face on the circle. Have students use the clock face and art supplies to design a "truly cuckoo" clock—a clock that is as unusual and creative as possible. Display the clocks on a table near the heading *"Truly Cuckoo" Clocks!*

MATERIALS
▲ small margarine lids
▲ construction paper
▲ crayons or markers
▲ scissors
▲ art supplies (cardboard tubes, pipe cleaners, boxes, construction paper, tagboard, yarn, elastic, buttons, feathers, etc.)
▲ tape
▲ glue

TAKE TIME FOR READ-ALOUDS

Celebrate Crazy Clock Day in a special way with this fun activity. Set an egg timer or alarm clock for the first hour of the morning, such as 9:00 a.m. When the timer or clock rings, gather the class in the reading corner and spend 10 minutes reading aloud. Explain that every hour on the hour for the rest of the day the class will gather for ten minutes to hear a continuation of a story or a new one. Reset the timer or clock for the next hour. During each meeting, discuss the passage of time; ask questions such as *Did the hour go by quickly or slowly? Why? Is 10 minutes shorter or longer than an hour?* or *How many hours have we been in school today?*

CRAZY TIMES

Print on several sentence strips sentences that describe events that take place at abnormal times, such as *I ate breakfast at 2:30* or *I went to bed for the night at 4:30.* Give students clocks with movable hands. Display a sentence strip, read it, and invite a volunteer to tell you what is wrong. Have volunteers share their suggestions. Then ask students to move the hands on their clocks to show a more normal time. Continue the activity with the rest of the sentence strips. Students have a great time fixing those crazy times!

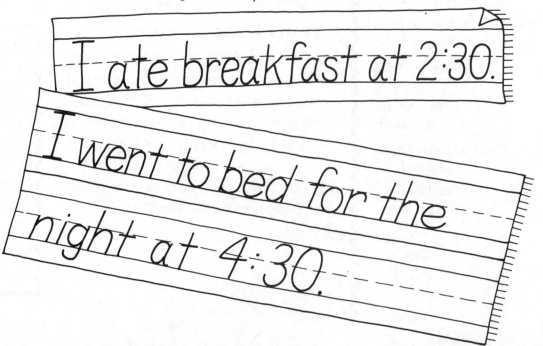

CHILI DAY

With October comes chilly mornings, chilly evenings, and chili suppers! Take the chill out of your students' autumn days by celebrating Chili Day—they'll have some "five-alarm" fun!

LITERATURE LINKS

The Big Stew
by Ben Schecter

Chile Pot
by Frederick Hayes and Jen Hayes

Cooking the Mexican Way
by Rosa Coronado

The Hamburger Book: All about Hamburgers and Hamburger Cooking
by Lila Perl

Mexican Food and Drink
by Manuel Alvarado

Soup for Supper
by Phyllis Root

When I eat some crackers,
I always have some chili.
It makes me feel so good.
It makes me feel so silly.

SILLY CHILI CLASS BOOK

Invite each student to think of a food that tastes good with chili and write the following sentence frame on a piece of construction paper: *When I eat some (type of food), I always have some chili. It makes me feel so good. It makes me feel so silly!* Invite students to cut the shape of their chosen food from construction paper and decorate it. Have students trace around a small margarine lid onto construction paper and cut out the circle. Instruct students to decorate the circle to look like their face and cut out a large mouth. Ask students to place glue around the circumference of the back side of the circle and glue it to the construction paper. (The mouth area should not be glued to the paper.) Invite students to push their food shape into the mouth on the circle. Have students use art supplies to add details such as hair, an upper body, a table, and a bowl of chili. Bind the papers in a class book titled *Silly Chili*.

MATERIALS
▲ construction paper
▲ crayons or markers
▲ small margarine lids
▲ scissors
▲ glue
▲ art supplies (yarn, buttons, craft sticks, construction-paper scraps, fabric scraps, etc.)

Chili Day

HODGEPODGE CHILI

Send home a note that invites each student to bring in an ingredient or topping for "hodgepodge" chili. Ingredients could include cooked ground meat, kidney beans, onions, green peppers, chili seasoning, or corn. Toppings could include sour cream, shredded cheese, cottage cheese, crackers, or chopped green onions. Make the chili together in the morning and let it simmer until afternoon. Invite each student to have a bowl of chili and add toppings of his or her choice. Read *Chile Pot* aloud as students enjoy their treat!

CHILI BEAN RELAY

Divide the class into equal-size relay teams. Mark a start and "turnaround" line with tape or chalk. Have teams line up behind the start line. Give each student a spoon to hold between his or her teeth. Place a dry kidney bean on the spoon of the first player of each team. Say *Go* and invite the players to walk to the turnaround line and back without dropping the bean or spoon. (If players drop the bean, they must place it back on the spoon and continue.) Have players pass the bean to their teammates as they return to the start line. The first team to complete the relay wins.

BAT DAY

Bats are the only flying mammals! Some bats migrate like birds do; others hibernate during the winter for up to 80 days! Use the following activities to help your students learn about these fascinating creatures—they'll go "batty" over them!

LITERATURE LINKS

A Bat Is Born
by Randall Jarrell

The Bat Poet
by Randall Jarrell

Lavina Bat
by Russell Hoban

Rufus
by Tomi Ungerer

Spooky and the Wizard's Bats
by Nathan Carlson

Stellaluna
by Janell Cannon

PAPER-SACK BATS

Read aloud and discuss *Stellaluna.* Make a class list of bat facts from the back of the story. Then invite each student to make a paper-sack bat. Have each student use white crayon to write a bat fact on a black lunch sack. Have students stuff the sacks with newspaper and tie the tops with string. Instruct them to cut bat wings from brown or black construction paper and tape the wings to the sacks. Invite students to design a construction-paper face for their bat, cut out the face, and glue it to the sack. Instruct students to break a toothpick in half and glue it to the bat's mouth for teeth. Tie string to the top of the bats and hang them from the ceiling.

MATERIALS
- ▲ *Stellaluna* by Janell Cannon
- ▲ black lunch sacks
- ▲ newspaper
- ▲ string
- ▲ scissors
- ▲ crayons or markers
- ▲ brown or black construction paper
- ▲ tape
- ▲ toothpicks
- ▲ glue

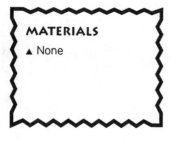

MATERIALS
▲ None

BATS ARE SLEEPING

Teach, and have students practice singing, the following song. Invite students to perform the song during an October assembly or for other classes.

Bats Are Sleeping
(to the tune of "Are You Sleeping?")

Bats are sleeping, bats are sleeping.
Upside down, upside down.
Sleeping in the morning sun.
Waiting for the night to come.
Then they fly, all around.

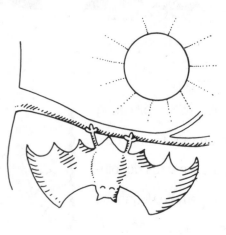

MATERIALS
▲ Bat reproducible (page 85)
▲ crayons or markers
▲ tagboard
▲ scissors
▲ glue
▲ pennies
▲ toothpicks

BALANCE THE BAT

Have each student color the Bat reproducible, glue it to tagboard, and cut it out. Invite students to tape a penny to each wing. Ask students to glue a toothpick vertically down the center of the bat. Challenge students to balance the head of the bat (where the toothpick is located) on the tip of their finger while they make it fly up and down by raising and lowering their hand.

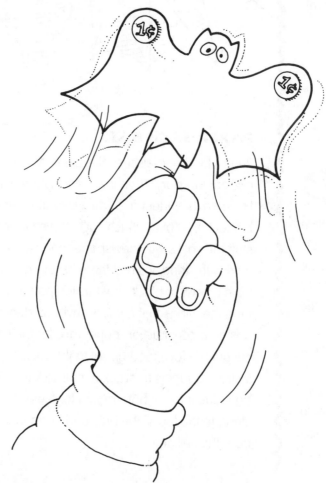

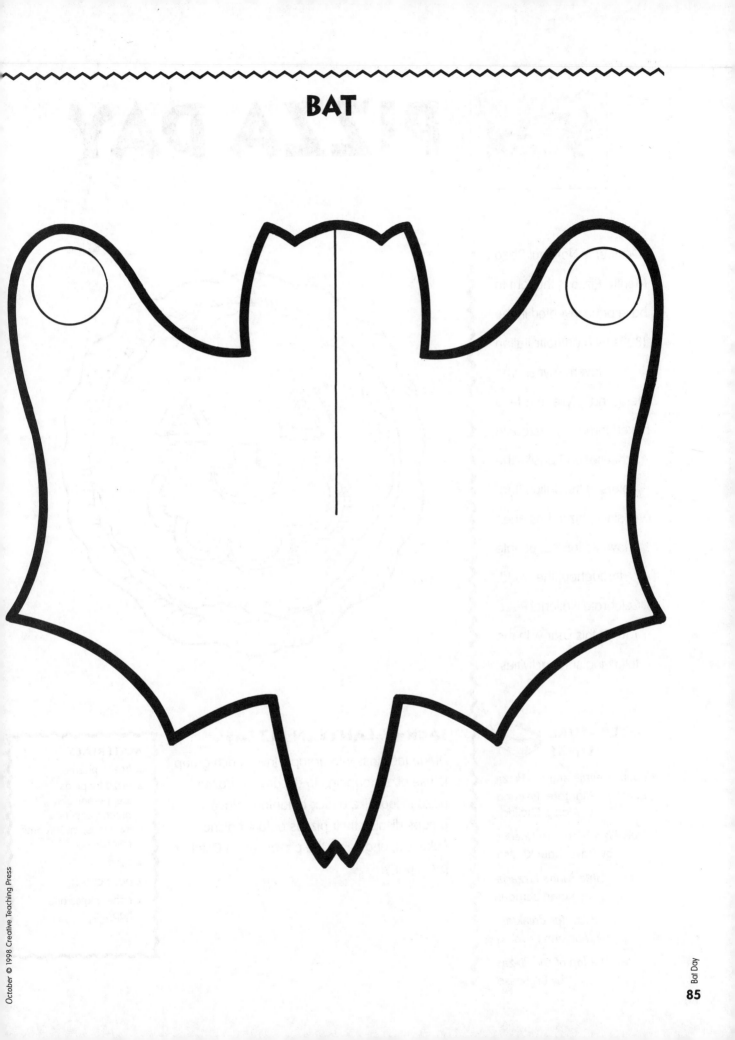

PIZZA DAY

October is National Pizza Month! Pizza is thought to have been invented in the 1800s by a patriotic Italian tavern owner who designed a "pie" made of baked tomato, mozzarella cheese, and basil—the colors of the Italian flag! Ever since, pizza has been a favorite food of people throughout the world. Celebrate National Pizza Month this year with the following spicy activities.

LITERATURE LINKS

Curious George and the Pizza edited by Margaret Rey and Alan J. Shalleck

How Pizza Came to Queens by Dayal Kaur Khalsa

Little Nino's Pizzaria by Karen Barbour

Pizza for Breakfast by Maryann Kovalski

The Top of the Pizzas by Bill Basso

JACK-O'-LANTERN PIZZAS

Divide the class into groups. Invite each group to use pizza toppings to decorate a frozen pizza to look like a jack-o'-lantern. Have groups display their pizzas before baking. Bake, cut, and serve the pizzas for an October pizza party!

MATERIALS
▲ frozen pizzas
▲ pizza toppings (pepperoni, olives, green peppers, tomatoes, mushrooms, onions)
▲ oven
▲ pizza cutter
▲ paper plates and napkins

PIZZA POEMS

MATERIALS
▲ pizza book (see Literature Links, page 86)
▲ construction-paper circles
▲ crayons or markers

Read aloud and discuss a pizza book. Then invite students to follow the pattern below and write a five-line "pizza poem" in the center of a construction-paper circle. Invite students to decorate around their poems with drawings of pizza toppings.

Pizza
Round, cheesy
Tossing, baking, melting
One piece isn't enough
Yummy treat!

Line	Poetry Description	Example
1	one-word title	Pizza
2	two words that describe the title	Round, cheesy
3	three action words	Tossing, baking, melting
4	four words that describe feelings	One piece isn't enough
5	word or words that mean the same as the title	Yummy treat!

"FAVORITE TOPPING" GRAPH

MATERIALS
▲ butcher-paper graph
▲ construction-paper triangles
▲ crayons or markers
▲ stapler
▲ tape

Make a large butcher-paper bar graph as shown. Hang the graph on the wall or a bulletin board. Invite each student to write his or her name on a construction-paper triangle and decorate around the name so the triangle resembles a slice of pizza. Have each student tape the triangle on the graph to show which topping is his or her favorite. Discuss the graph; ask questions such as *Which is the favorite topping? Which is the least favorite?* or *How many more/fewer people are there who like pepperoni than there are people who like mushrooms?*

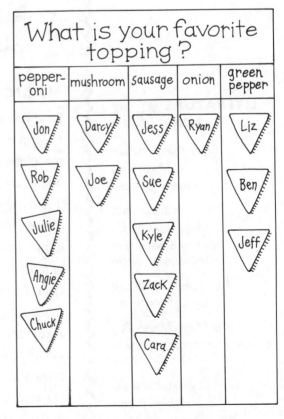

What is your favorite topping?

pepper-oni	mushroom	sausage	onion	green pepper
Jon	Darcy	Jess	Ryan	Liz
Rob	Joe	Sue		Ben
Julie		Kyle		Jeff
Angie		Zack		
Chuck		Cara		

MAGIC DAY

Fourth Week of October

The fourth week of October marks National Magic Week—a perfect time to bring some magic into your classroom! Invite your students to experience some tricks and treats with the following activities. Your students will have a "magical" time!

LITERATURE LINKS

MAGIC BREW

Send home a note that invites students to bring in one of the following ingredients in a resealable plastic bag: peanuts without shells (magic beans), candy corn (fall corn), M&Ms (eye of newt), Chex cereal (spider webs), raisins (troll buttons), shoestring potato crisps (scarecrow straw), straight pretzels (magic wands), miniature marshmallows (ghost noses). Have students add the ingredients to a black plastic pot. Stir the pot and invite students to chant *Abracadabra, Alacazam, make this brew as fast as you can. One, two, three, poof!* Take the "magic brew" to an out-of-the-way table and pour it into cups that have a small toy or sticker at the bottom. (Be sure students cannot see the surprises.) Serve the brew and watch the looks of surprise when they find that a treat has magically appeared in the magic brew.

MATERIALS

- ▲ resealable plastic bags
- ▲ food brought from home
- ▲ black plastic pot
- ▲ wooden spoon
- ▲ plastic cups
- ▲ small toys or stickers

MAGIC STAR

Invite students to perform an easy magic trick that they can take home and share with family and friends. Have each student fold five toothpicks in half without breaking them. Ask students to place them on a shallow plate, as shown. Invite students to pour water from a measuring cup on the toothpicks until the toothpicks move to form a star. Amazing!

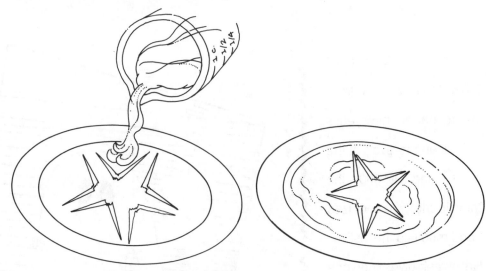

MAGIC "MONEY BOX" TRICKS

Read aloud *The Magic Money Box.* Invite student pairs to decorate a shoe box with construction paper and crayons or markers to make a "magic money box." Give each pair several pennies, nickels, dimes, and quarters with which to perform "magic tricks" like those described in the book. For a "demonstration round," have pairs put all the coins but the pennies in their box. Have one partner from each pair be the magician, place five pennies in the box, say *Five pennies go in the box,* and tap the box with a pencil (magic wand). Have the other partner be the assistant, pull a nickel from the box, and say *One nickel comes out, tah-dah!* Invite pairs to work with the coins and develop two similar "magic tricks" with other coins. Have each pair perform the tricks for the class.

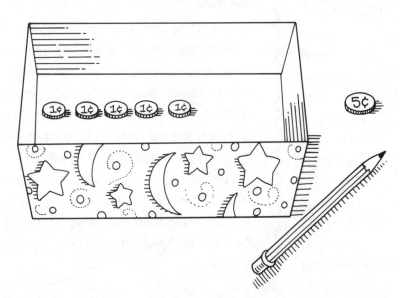

HALLOWEEN

October 31

Halloween developed from several ancient new year's festivals and festivals of the dead. In the A.D. 800s, the Catholic church recognized and modified the festival. Halloween gives everyone the chance to dress up in costume, go to parties, and assume another identity for a little while. Your students can, too!

LITERATURE LINKS

Apples and Pumpkins
by Ann Rockwell

Dorrie and the Wizard's Spell
by Patricia Coombs

Four on the Shore
by Edward Marshall

Guess What?
by Mem Fox

Halloween
by Gail Gibbons

Halloween
by Joyce K. Kessel

MOSTLY GHOSTLY HALLOWEEN CARDS

Have each student fold a piece of black construction paper in half to make a card. Invite students to paint one of their hands white and press it (upside down) on the card. When the paint dries, ask students to paint two black eyes near the top of the hand print. Invite students to use white crayon and write Halloween messages inside the card such as *Have a "boo-tiful" Halloween* or *Have a frightfully fun Halloween!* Have students take home the cards and present them to family or friends.

MATERIALS
▲ black construction paper
▲ white and black tempera paint/ paintbrushes
▲ white crayon

HALLOWEEN OWLS

Invite each student to fold a piece of brown construction paper into three sections so the middle section is twice as large as the two sides. Ask students to draw two owl wings on the two side sections, filling only the bottom two-thirds of each side (see illustration). Have students cut out around the wings, leaving them attached to the middle section. Instruct students to draw an owl's head on the top third of the middle section so the head pokes over the wings when the wings are folded. Ask students to cut around the owl's head. Then invite students to write on the owl's body a short story or poem about an owl on Halloween. Have students fold the wings to cover the completed stories or poems. Display the owls on a bulletin board titled *Hooting about Halloween!*

EDUCATIONAL COSTUME PARTY

Instead of a traditional "choose your own costume" Halloween party, turn your class Halloween party into a learning event. Choose an "educational" theme for the party, such as community helpers and careers, favorite book characters, famous inventors and scientists, presidents and first ladies, the Revolutionary War, Noah's Ark, or costumes depicting beings and objects of one color. Send home a note that asks students to read (at home) nonfiction books about the theme and design a costume based on someone or something they have read about. (Be sure to send home the note early in the month so families have time to prepare.) Invite students to wear the themed costumes during the party. Have the class guess at the beginning of the party whom each student is dressed like.

OCTOBER

SUNDAY	MONDAY	TUESDAY	WEDNESDAY	THURSDAY	FRIDAY	SATURDAY

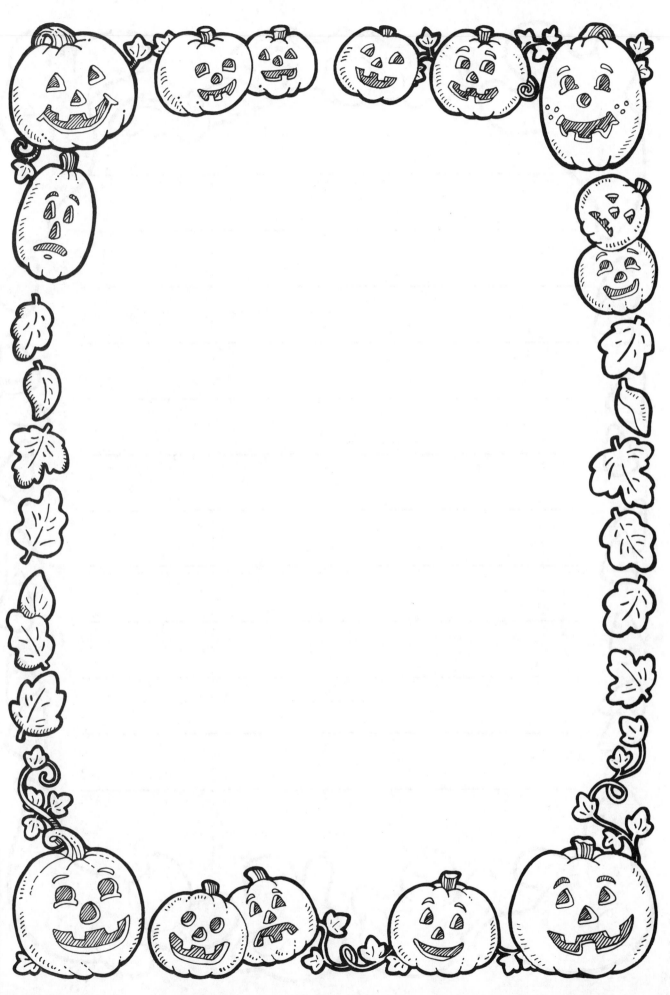

Pumpkin Border

October News

October Newsletter